"HONEY, IT'S ALL IN THE SHOES"

"HONEY, IT'S ALL IN THE SHOES"

Celebrating the Footsteps of the Contemporary Woman

Phyllis Norton Hoffman

Health Communications, Inc.
Deerfield Beach, Florida

www.hcibooks.com

Library of Congress Cataloging-in-Publication Data

Hoffman, Phyllis.

    Honey, it's all in the shoes! : celebrating the footsteps of the contemporary woman/ Phyllis Hoffman.

      p. cm.

    ISBN-13: 978-0-7573-0757-7

    ISBN-10: 0-7573-0757-4

    1. Women's shoes—Social aspects.   2. Hoffman, Phyllis.   I. Title.

    GT2130.H64 2009

    391.4'13082—dc22

2009014461

© 2009 Phyllis Norton Hoffman

Publisher: Health Communications, Inc.
        3201 S.W. 15th Street
        Deerfield Beach, FL 33442–8190

Cover photo ©Photodisc Photography
Interior illustrations © Marie Barber
Cover, interior design and formatting by Lawna Patterson Oldfield

This book is dedicated to my twin sons, Eric and Brian, who make my steps worth taking every day. Raising you was a pleasure, working with you is rewarding, loving you is effortless, and sharing life with you is my heart's desire.

Eric, your witty smile and sparkling eyes always tell me you are up to something! Your eyes are the window to your soul, and in them, I find love, joy, seriousness, challenge, integrity, and loyalty. As you are beginning your new role as a father, I am so moved by your desire to be the best dad you can be to Hays. I love you, my son.

Brian, your laughter fills the room. Your quick wit and entertaining spirit fill each day with joy. Your smile is always contagious and your love is unconditional. I have watched you grow into a man who people love being with. You challenge me to be a better person, and your love overwhelms me at times. I love you, my son.

Although twins, both of you are mirror opposites of each other in so many ways. It's as though you are two sides of the same coin, or two puzzle pieces that fit together seamlessly to create the perfect picture of sons. I love you both so much and wish you all the happiness the world can offer. God blessed my life in the most extraordinary way when he gave you to me.

CONTeNTS

PROLOGUe

Honey, It's All in the Shoes

I was recently on the Internet and ran across a web page that listed the "Rules for Southern Belles." As the publisher of *Southern Lady* magazine and a born-and-bred Southerner, I couldn't help but pause and read these "rules" with interest. They included advisories to "never show anger in public" or never "chew gum or smoke on the street." The writer's well-intended words also urge budding young belles to always write thank-you notes and to "charm, charm, charm." But the number-one rule that all Southern ladies are expected to abide by—and this simply can't be written or stated often enough—is "never wear white shoes before Easter or after Labor Day." The author of the web page rightfully noted that the *only* exception to this rule is a bride on her wedding day. This so-called rule about white shoes is actually more of an inviolable code among Southern women. I have always wondered where it came from, and for the life of me, I couldn't tell you. I can only tell you that I have never, ever met a Southern woman who hasn't heard it her entire life.

In the South, shoes are a subject of much discussion, fascination, and decorum. For instance, we would no more ask a woman her age than her shoe size. It would be unmannerly! The fundamental rules of good breeding in the South also dictate that your shoes should always match the hem of your garment, and that your hose should never be darker than your shoes. Any Southern woman worth her red lipstick knows that shoes are important from a fashion standpoint. They make an outfit. I've always known that, of course; Southern women are raised on it. But what they might not know is that shoes are a common metaphor for all women, and for the footsteps of our lives. There is a reason why women have been obsessed with footwear for as many centuries as we can account for. For one thing, we are, first and foremost, creatures of the heart, and shoes allow us to fall in love over and over again! And like love, they make us feel. Our shoes change with our moods, the seasons, and with the different paths—both planned and otherwise—which our lives take.

Honey, It's All in the Shoes (my personal slogan) started out being a simple little tell-all about my favorite fashion fetish and ended up being a book that has surprised even me. Until I sat down at the computer, started writing, and truly connected the dots, it hadn't occurred to me that my favorite accessory is more than just matching the perfect pair of shoes to an outfit. Now don't get me wrong, that matters! When I meet another woman, the first thing I look at is her shoes. Does the color work with the rest of her ensemble, is the shoe's silhouette especially striking, how high is the heel, or does the peep-toe show off her pedicure to perfection? But this book is more than just a diary of my shoe obsession; it is an extension of my passion for exploring the multi-faceted elements of femininity, and for sharing those discoveries with other women.

Just as no two women share the same shoe closet, no two women share the same exact life experiences. But it is our commonalities that interest me most. Women, as a rule, tend to love shoes, because they are an outer expression of who we are inside, at least for that moment. It is both the privilege and the prerogative of every woman to change her shoes as often as she changes her mind or her mood! I never dreamed I would write a book about my shoes or my footsteps in them along the way and over the years. When I was a little girl, I dreamed about becoming many things. I wanted someday to be a gracious woman, a true Southern lady in the tradition of my mother and her mother before her. I wanted to be as funny and flippant as Lucille Ball, as fashionable as Jackie Kennedy, and as audacious as Scarlett O'Hara.

> I did not have three thousand pairs of shoes. I had one thousand and sixty.
> —Imelda Marcos

I grew up to be a publisher of magazines and books; a mother and grandmother; a Harley Davidson-riding, piano-playing, certified shoe fanatic who is lucky enough to have the opportunity to share a little of my lifelong infatuation with footwear and a few of my stories with you. I dedicate each page to all the Southern ladies out there—regardless of your geography—and to every woman who is struggling, even a little, to find her way. I wish you well on your quest and I invite you to examine mine with me in *Honey, It's All About the Shoes*. More than anything, it is my most sincere hope that you find the perfect pair of shoes to take you wherever life takes you next. You never know where that might be or what it might entail, but the right shoes can, and do, make all the difference in getting there!

CHAPTER 1

Shoes for the Journey

G rowing up in an average American family in Birmingham, Alabama, the oldest of three children, I had dreams of becoming what every young Southern girl hopes she will someday be. I longed to become a wonderful wife and mother and a woman of substance and style, a woman who is sure of herself and the image she wants to always portray through the clothing she wears, the words she chooses, and her actions towards others. Well honey, I can tell you, I never expected to find myself here: a woman in midlife steering a $50 million publishing company while navigating life changes; the mother of handsome, grown, twin sons who are setting out on journeys of their own; an employer to nearly 200 people; a friend to some wonderful

and influential women you probably have heard of, like
Nancy Grace, Sandra Lee, Dixie Carter, and Paula Deen, and
others whose names you may not know but whom I treasure
as dearly as diamonds. I think that's what women are—we
are diamonds, rare and precious jewels, multifaceted, and
always mysterious, and I have devoted my entire adult life
to exploring in print our inner and outer lives, publishing
such magazines as *Southern Lady, Victoria, Sandra Lee Semi-
Homemade, Cooking with Paula Deen, TeaTime,* and *Taste of the
South.*

My career has been built on the idea that you can tell a
lot about the inner thoughts of a woman through her out-
ward expressions—her taste in wardrobe, how she decorates
her home, the meals she prepares for herself or her family,
how much care and time she takes being gracious and hos-
pitable to others. You will see all of those elements in the
magazines we produce at Hoffman Media; they are reflections of a woman's personality. In this book, I am taking on
a single aspect of the feminine panorama I have adored and
explored for more than twenty-five years now: Shoes. Why?
Because I love them, of course, but also because I believe that
shoes are so utterly iconic to our daily lives as women, and
through them, we connect to each other. The majority of
the time, women dress for other women, not for men, and I
believe that shoes, and the footsteps we take in them, are our
common link, a way for us to get to know, appreciate, and
even mentor one another as women.

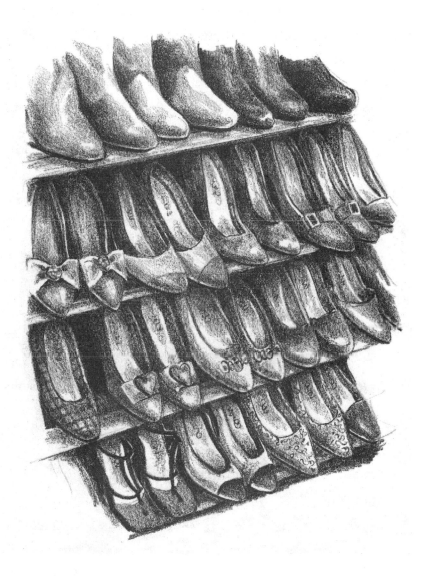

Shoes are more than mere fashion accessories—they are metaphors for a woman's life, and for me, they are a happy obsession. Women are unique among God's creations; we mark the milestones of our lives with feminine totems that symbolize each precious stage of our development. For some women it is jewelry—I have a dear friend who has oodles of brooches, ranging in value, but each with a special memory attached to it—and for others it is purses or hats. For me it is shoes, and it has been since the very beginning. For instance, though I can't tell you what song was playing, I *can* tell you exactly what pair of shoes I was wearing when I first went to church and discovered a lifelong love of music. And though I'm not sure what was served in the cafeteria for lunch that day, I remember with perfect clarity the shoes I was wearing the first day of school. Junior high dances, senior proms, college entrance exams, first job, the birth of my sons, the conception of my career and company, and the weddings and (sadly) the funerals of friends and loved ones—all are organized in the calendar of my memory not by day or month or year, but by the style, fit, and color of the shoes I was wearing at the time.

What makes a woman tick? I'm still finding out. What makes *me* tick? I'm definitely still finding out—and part of my journey towards that discovery is writing this book. As women, we are always in transition. From the time we are young girls with uncharted dreams, we think we know exactly where we're going, but then, on any given day, along comes a phone call, an e-mail, a letter, or even a conversation that changes everything, and we find our circumstances setting our course instead of the other way around. I've lived long enough to know that while I can't always be sure of where I am going, I know for certain where I have been, and looking back on those footsteps gives me fresh perspective, even hope. I have so much to share with other women who may be traveling on some of those same roads and asking some of the same questions that have confronted me in my life, and shoes seem to me the perfect metaphor for the journey!

Aside from my wonderful family, my friends, and my readers, I am quite simply in love with shoes! I would rather have a new pair of shoes than almost anything. When my world weighs heavy on my shoulders or when I simply need a little lift, I head for my shoe closet. Shoes are the perfect tonic for whatever ails me. As you'll learn throughout the book, shoes offer me comfort when I need it, adventure when I crave it, motivation when I lack it, and humor when I wish for a lift in my spirits.

My closet is truly a sanctuary where I keep the things that are most precious and personal to me. I open the double French doors and immediately, the cares of my heart are truly lessened and lifted as I start trying on pair after pair, until I find the perfect ones to suit (or change) my mood. On the shelves that line the walls, my shoes are grouped neatly by color or heel height. Some days I'll reach for a pair of three-inch stilettos in a "hello world" color, but other days may be more of a two-inch Palin pump kind of day, where I am, either by necessity or mood, more business and less play.

Now, a stranger might open my closet doors and see little more than a chaotic sea of T-straps, buckles, and bows. Not me. I see memories, possibilities, dreams, secret wishes, dear friends, and loved ones with faces so familiar I can close my eyes and count every laugh line, every freckle, every furrow. I see the framed photograph of my beloved friend Dr. Steve Davis that I keep here always. Steve was the greatest practical joker of all time (second to me, of course), and he was ravaged by cancer and robbed of his life when he was far too young. The shoes I was wearing the last time I saw him are here in my closet, as well as the black pumps I wore to his funeral. I like to think dear Steve is watching over my shoes, and me, from heaven.

A pair of lethal red stacks chosen by my son Brian sit at eye level, while on an opposite shelf, the scrumptious chocolate brown satin slingbacks I wore to his twin brother Eric's wedding sit waiting to be worn again. I didn't think about shoes when I dashed like an Olympic sprinter to the hospital last year for the birth of Eric's son (and my first grandson), but if I'd had time to change, I might have. Like all good Southern women, I love a poetic moment even more than a great pair of heels! There are so many memories here in my shoe closet, not to mention a few new beginnings.

My most recent acquisitions are still in the box. They are my official "starting over" shoes picked out by Barbara Cockerham, my best friend in the world and the talented editor of *Victoria* and *TeaTime*. They are a medium heel slingback with a striking black and white print and an elegant red grosgrain double bow. I never imagined I would be forced to reinvent myself in my fifties, or that my path would so radically shift course from the one I started out on so long ago. But new paths call for new shoes. Being single at 55 after an unanticipated divorce has taken me down a path I never expected to walk.

In my shoe closet, I see my life so clearly. I see the people I have known until now, the places I've been, and the places I hope to someday visit—because when I finally get there, you can be certain I will be wearing *fabulous* shoes. The shoes in my collection represent more than a lifelong obsession with style and presentation—though that is real enough. On a grander scale, and a higher plane, each pair of peep-toe pumps or strappy, mile-high sandals represents the milestone in my life, a footstep I've taken, the people who have taken that walk with me, and the things I've learned along the way.

My shoes have always been a part of that journey, and since feminine footwear is a multimillion-dollar industry, I think it's safe to say the same is true for a great many other women as well! And while I acquiesce to those who say getting there is half the fun of life's journey, I have to add one tiny caveat: Getting there in to-die-for shoes is even more fun! Don't you think that's true? In the South, it certainly is. Match the wrong shoes to the right dress or handbag and we will all have a good laugh! Shoes matter. They show to the world that you take pride in your appearance and in yourself, and more important, they are part of a woman's armor. Even when our hearts are breaking or we are so scared we feel like our skin will come right *off*, a great pair of shoes can ground us.

As a little girl, each new pair of shoes was marked by the occasion—church on Sundays, Easter, or Christmas. Growing up, I didn't need more than three pair of shoes at any given time or season: a pretty pair for Sundays and such, a sturdy pair for play, and an everyday pair for school. Outgrowing shoes was the focus then, so I was exceedingly happy when my feet settled into one size and acquiring new shoes became not a necessity but rather a pastime, one of pure pleasure. I remember the first time I ever saw a pair of shoes and thought, "I want *those*." I was a young girl and the shoes in question belonged to my late grandmother Bernice Norton. They were cherry red platform heels that matched her handbag and lipstick, and they were gorgeous. When Grandmother Norton wore them, she looked like everything a Southern lady could hope to be: beautiful, remarkably stylish, and absolutely fearless about wherever she was headed next. That was when I discovered the *magic* of shoes and where they could take a woman, both literally and figuratively.

> Yes, only a shoe, but if I provide escape for the woman who wears it, if for only a few minutes, it brings a bit of happiness to someone, well, then, perhaps, it is something more than a shoe.
>
> —Manolo Blahnik

There are special times in my life that I remember by way of the shoes I wore. First day of school? Black patent Mary Janes. First job interview? Black leather pumps with a no-nonsense, two-inch heel. When I was carrying my wonderful twin boys? The flattest flats I could find, of course! Footwear, whether pointed-toe heels or tennis shoes, mark time in a woman's life and tells you a story about each step along the way. French foodie and philosopher Jean Anthelme Brillat-Savarin very famously said, "Tell me what you eat and I'll tell you what you are." By the same token, show me your shoes and I'll tell you about your personality, perhaps even a thing or two you didn't think anyone noticed or knew.

Shoes make a statement about your personality, and even, more simply, your mood. Shoes are about attitude. When I put on a pair of snazzy shoes, I have attitude! The perfect shoe for me is a red, sling-back medium heel pump, especially if I am going to be walking in them all day. They are pretty as you please, but also prim, proper, and to the point. I have been known, on occasion, to summon up an extra little bit of courage and confidence with a knock-out pair of what I like to call "valet shoes." You know just what I'm talking about, I bet. These beauties are the private reserve of shoes—they are strictly for show. Valet shoes are meant to be worn from the car into your destination, where you must proceed to the nearest chair to sit down. You'd best stay down too, because the pain of your fanciful footwear will override all sense of style after one hour!

As women, our shoes define so much about us, from the time our feet first hit the ground running in baby booties, to wobbling around knock-kneed on our first pair of heels, to becoming old and wise enough to know when to take off the pinchy pumps, kick back, and let our bare toes tickle through the grass for a while.

Isn't that part of a journey all women share? Don't you look at your own footprints and wonder what happened to the wishes you held so dear as a girl, when you could only dream of filling a pair of woman-sized shoes? You start out on your path in one pair of shoes with one set of expectations, then everything shifts along the way. There is discovery, yes, and new shoes to try on, which is exciting. But you may find, as I have, that some shoes aren't as snug as they were when you first put them on and that others have become scuffed and worn and should be discarded along with the pieces of yourself that no longer serve or suit you. But, happily, there are also those shoes that go the distance; that, if properly cared for and frequently worn, will last a lifetime. Those are the best kind.

My shoes have definitely marked me. They tell you who I am, who I was, and they give you an inkling of who I just might become. I hope by peeking into my shoe closets past and present, you learn a thing or two about your own life, how to examine it, and celebrate it—with glorious acceptance and satisfaction. A great man once said that the life unexamined is not worth living. Very true. I happen to believe, and have long advocated, that women can and do examine their lives every day when they open their closets. What's inside those closets is very telling about who we are as individuals, and a closer inspection can remind us of things we may have forgotten (by design or otherwise) while mirroring who we are inside and pinpointing us on our inner roadmaps. Your shoes help you take stock of yourself and your life, and I invite you to join me on this leg of my journey, as I continue on the unexpected, sometimes painful, but always interesting path that I have chosen. (Or maybe the path chose me. I'm still not sure.) What I know for a fact is this: My closet is full, and so is my life. Honey, it *is* all in the shoes, and I'm so glad you're willing to walk a mile or two in mine with me. Let's go!

SPiKe HeeLS

Dagger-like stiletto heels first became wildly popular in the 1950s and 1960s thanks to celebrated shoe designer Roger Vivier, who described his frequently extravagant shoe designs as "sculptures." Critics and fans were even more complimentary, calling his couture creations the "Faberge of Footwear." His cutting-edge shoes were feathered, bejeweled, and otherwise embellished, earning Vivier a lasting reputation as a one-of-a-kind artist. Of his work he said, "To be carried by shoes, winged by them, to wear dreams on one's feet, is to begin to give reality to one's dreams."

The Frenchman was the most in-demand and celebrated shoe designer of his era—he even fashioned the gold kidskin shoes worn by Queen Elizabeth II at her coronation in 1953. But he is undoubtedly best remembered for the spike heel. Working with haute couturier Christian Dior, Vivier created spike heels specifically to comple- ment the clothing designer's glamorous day and evening wear lines. Vivier's stilettos were most typically three to four inches in height and tapered to as little as three-eighths of an inch in diameter; each pair was reinforced with a metal rod for support and to help prevent the needle-like heel from snapping in half.

CHAPTER 2

In the Beginning

In the beginning, I only had one pair of shoes to choose from. I can't imagine I liked that very much, and I'm certain that I must have frowned at those shoes with disdain when my mother shoved me into them every day. A single pair of shoes to go with every outfit? The idea is so foreign and outrageous to me, I shudder just thinking about it! And they were white, no less—you don't wear white after Labor Day, despite current propaganda that is spread from popular cable makeover shows. Every Southern woman knows that, for heaven's sake, but that's another subject. Footwear for babies has, thankfully, become a little more fashion-forward in the decades since my first pair was chosen for me. When my sons started walking, I had more walking shoe options than my mother had in her day, and now that my unbelievably handsome, obviously brilliant, incredibly engaging grandson has been born, there are even more cute-as-a-button shoes to choose from.

The most remarkable thing about my first walkers is that I have absolutely no memory of them. In fact, it is only from family photo albums and framed portraits that I know about them. They were pristine white in color, with hardy leather soles and no-nonsense high-topped uppers. Thick, ropy laces weaved in and out through a series of eyeholes and hooks and snugly tied together at the tops, which hugged my calves, and which were, at the time, proportionate to my wobbly ankles. Though not terribly sleek or elegant, my orthopedic-style baby shoes were the reigning fashion for toddlers at the time (the 1950s for those who simply *must* know). What's more, they were commensurate to the task to which they were appointed.

Chosen for me by my mother, who laced me into them with her loving hands, those shoes were the fashion equivalent of what the Romans might have called a *tabula rasa*, which is to say a "blank slate." They were not designed to be especially pretty—though they weren't particularly objectionable, merely bland. Those little white shoes were made to perform, to support and protect my untested, tender little feet as I made the transition from crawling like an infant to standing on my own. That's a lot to ask of a shoe. And while I know now that walking in those little white shoes way back then could not have been easy, learning to do so set the tone for challenges that were to come later in life, learning yet again to walk at each new turn, stumbling innocently along foreign paths of new life stages.

Though I can't recall my own first steps, they were surely as shaky and wide-eyed as those of any other toddler. I imagine that I looked into my mother's eyes with perfect love and trust, clutching her hands with all my might as I pulled myself to a trembling stance. I can't recall, but I'm certain that I did not entirely believe her when she no doubt told me I *could* walk, I *could*, I *could*. But with the patience and love only a mother can know or understand, she somehow coaxed me forward into a hesitant lifting and falling of the feet, which must have became a steadier gait with each subsequent step. As a baby, there you are in shoes that someone picked for you and put on your feet. As you take one trembling step after the other, you are buffered by boundaries of love that you don't even know are there until you cross them. Hands hold you up, then, almost without your notice, slip away and let you go it on your own, all the while hovering protectively just steps behind you, ready to catch you if you fall. Those fledgling steps were the beginnings of my own unique path—they set the pace for a lifetime of exploration, running to and from people, places, and things; tripping over myself more than once; facing and overcoming

obstacles; and ultimately staying steady on my feet and moving forward.

No matter the circumstances or even the individual, isn't
life really just a series of baby steps for all of us? As a woman,
I have taken so many first steps I have lost count—sometimes
without stumbling and other times falling flat on my face!
But each time, I got back up, put one foot in front of the
other, and kept going; women are nothing if not resilient! I
suspect that we never really leave our first walkers behind,
that the shoes in which we take those first few trembling
steps simply change size and shape and style as we grow
older. One pair that stands out in my mind
were not even "shoes" at all—they were
house slippers, and I wore them in
the spring of 1981, when I was 27
and expecting twins.

> It isn't the
> mountain ahead
> that wears you out;
> it's the grain of sand
> in your shoe.
> —Rodan of Alexandria

It was a glorious time in my life; I
was a newlywed living in Cullman,
Alabama, with my husband, Wayne. I
loved being a wife and wanted more than
anything to be a mother too. And even though other people
thought I was crazy, I prayed for twins. I figured that if one
baby was a blessing, two would be doubly so, and I was totally
right! Of course, wishing for twins was one thing—getting
them here turned out to be another matter. My OB-GYN,
Howard Williamson, told me that a multiple pregnancy was
sometimes complicated and that I would have to view those

nine months a little differently than other expecting mothers. I would have to slow down, be cautious. Me, are you kidding? I was in total heaven thinking about two babies. What did he know, I thought to myself. He was a man!

As the early months of the pregnancy progressed, I found myself eating healthfully and walking, just booking along as the typical, textbook mom-to-be. I kept up my regular pace as a homemaker, and kept right on working as a clinic administrator for Cullman Internal Medicine. And honey, let me tell you, I did it all wearing high heels. I was having a ball! Having gained only a few pounds, I was right on course for the perfect pregnancy, and I waited for those babies with nothing but joy in my heart. I bought two of everything—bassinets, blankets, onesies, and, of course, tiny little pure white shoes made of cloth.

While I was immersed in mommy bliss, though, Howard was watching me like a hawk. In early January, during a routine visit when I was four months pregnant, he told me that I would be removing the stilettos and staying off my feet until the babies came. I was scared to death, but I took a hiatus from work right after I finished the last tax return for the doctors I worked for. I stayed home, and I stayed put. I went from bed to couch for several weeks until one night; I felt an odd, persistent fluttering that made me nervous, so I called the doctor just to make sure that this was normal.

It was not. A quick trip to the hospital confirmed I was in labor. I was so terrified, but another friend, Tommy Baccus, was on call that night and he managed to control the labor with IV medications that slowed the contractions to a manageable level. I was so relieved and ready to chalk it all up to a close call, but Tommy informed me that he was keeping me in the hospital until Howard returned the following Monday. When he did, Howard made the call that I should finish out my pregnancy in the hospital, and I was only five months along!

I was completely in shock. Me? In the hospital for four months? I hadn't sat still for four *minutes* in my entire life! I am a person who is wide open all of the time, who is in the office before 8 AM and still on the phone long after 5. I have always been constantly on the go, forever creating some new this or that, always imagining a creative way for women to live their lives, incessantly in search of the next big *thing*. In business, I have always been pretty sure of my next step, but as a young mother-to-be, I suddenly found myself without a map, and forced to learn the meaning of the word "stop." Because I had the lives of my two unborn babies at stake, I did just that. I stopped. The next four months were spent nesting in my little hospital room. I decorated the walls with pictures, the shelves with plants and flowers, the tabletop with keepsakes. As we say in the South, I "made do," passing each long day as still and as stoic as I could stand. As a Southern woman, I had other daily concerns to busy myself with as well—specifically, my appearance. Luckily, I was prepared.

In my Southern family, you see, it is assumed that at some point, a trip to the hospital will be made, and there are three things that must be ever-present to ready one's self for the inevitable. First, Norton ladies are required to keep a suitcase ready to pack at all times, which is to include a presentable nightgown that is designed to cover you completely (no awkward gaps in the back, as with hospital gowns) while enhancing the color of your cheeks and eyes. The second is a lovely matching robe. The third is a great pair of house slippers, comfortable yet stylish. Because I had no way of knowing that my middle-of-the-night trip to the hospital would stretch into an eight-week stay, I had failed to bring my Norton family suitcase. So, on day one, Mom was kind enough to pack for me and bring me the shoes I had left behind at home, slippers that would come to symbolize so much to me before those boys were born and after they were placed into my waiting arms. They were white fuzzy slippers, and I wore them for my once-a-day walk down the hall, the only real escape from my room that I was afforded.

During my hospital stint, I stayed in labor for six weeks, until Eric and Brian were born five weeks premature. They were tiny little boys and my walks to the nursery became more frequent and fervent as I longed to see them and be near them. They were so small that they slept together in one of the plastic bassinets in the hospital nursery. I was frightened every time I made my way down the hall, and it wasn't until I made it to their makeshift crib and looked into their precious faces that my fear would begin to subside. I was so weak from the weeks of labor and the C-section delivery that I could hardly walk. The scuffling sound of my fuzzy white slippers on the gleaming, polished hospital floors seemed deafening to me each day as I made it slowly down the hallway, rounding the corners, and hoping to find two thriving little boys with the name "Hoffman" on the bassinet. "Complicated" was the word Howard had used and he was so right.

Ten days after delivery, we had all stabilized enough to go home. After months of being in bed and off my feet, I didn't want to leave in a wheelchair. I insisted on walking from my bed, past the nursery, down through the lobby and into the car, and I wanted to take that walk in the slippers my mother had brought me, the slippers that had carried me step by painful step each day to check on my precious sons.

Eric and Brian flanked me, carried by their respective nurses. With me leading the way in my fuzzy slippers, our little family must have looked like a parade going down Main Street as we tenderly made our way to the front entrance. I had arrived at the hospital wary and oblivious to the quickness with which life can change. Now I was leaving a grateful, humbled woman in a stylish matching gown and robe, hair teased to the hilt, makeup applied to perfection, wearing fuzzy house shoes, with two beautiful sons who would soon enough need shoes of their own. I was in such pain as I moved, but so exhilarated too! I was about to cross the finish line, and I can't imagine a more perfect pair of shoes for those first steps back out into the world. They were comfortable, they were cute as all get-out, and like any great pair of "first walkers," they had helped me get a firmer grip on the unsure ground beneath me. For me, it was the walk of a lifetime, and one of many "first steps" to come.

THe ART OF BRONZiNG

Bronzing statuary as a means of immortalizing people, places, and events is a centuries-old practice, but it was the Baby Boomers who made bronzing baby shoes one of the first and most tender relics of childhood—a trend that has stuck with us over generations. In its seventy-plus years of operation, the American Bronzing Company in Columbus, Ohio, remains one of the most successful companies of its kind—artists there have dipped and plated more than 14 million pairs of baby booties and average some 200,000 new sets a year. It was a mother, of course, who founded the business.

After spotting a pair of bronzed baby shoes in a department store in the 1930s and realizing what a hot property these unique mementos could become, former kindergarten teacher Violet Shinbach took a leap of faith and jumped into the bronzing business. Initially, she took orders not only through department stores, but also by going door to door. A savvy businesswoman who knew her clientele, she specifically targeted young families, looking for homes with swing sets in the backyard or abandoned tricycles in the driveway; business particularly boomed in the post-war years.

Today, baby shoes sent to American Bronzing Company are first assigned an identification number to track them: then they are sealed, shaped by hand, dipped, plated, buffed, polished, sprayed with lacquer, mounted to a base, and, finally, returned to the proud parents.

These days, baby shoes can be dipped not only in bronze or copper, but also in silver, pewter, porcelain, or even gold! What an amazing way to commemorate your children, and to preserve the memories of their precious first steps.

CHAPTER 3

The Sound of Music

W hen I was young, little girls and boys were sent to the nursery to play while older kids and parents went to "big church" to worship. I can remember whiling away the hour in nursery wondering what went on in this mysterious "big church" where I *never* got to go. It had to be fun. It had to be fabulous. It just *had* to be. My parents and all of their friends always came out of the chapel smiling and happy every Sunday, so I felt certain that it was good, whatever was going on in there, and cookies and milk in the nursery were little consolation for missing out on it.

I rejoiced when I *finally* turned five, outgrew the nursery, and made my premiere at big church. I wish I could tell you the message of the sermon that Sunday, but I can't. What I

remember is the music. I was enraptured by it. The hymns
were so beautiful, and even though I couldn't read the words
to sing along—and probably would not have entirely understood them even if I could have—God spoke to me through
the music itself. That Sunday, and every Sunday afterward, I
would sit on the church pew beside my parents, hold my
breath, and wait for the music to begin. Once the first notes
sounded, I kept my eyes trained on the organist and pianist,
watching how their fingers trilled across their keyboards,
sweeping over the keys with movements that were sometimes
delicate and at other times overtly dramatic, often within the
same song.

As I watched, it began to dawn on me that it was not only the organist's hands that moved, providing those wonderful sounds, but also her feet. What's more, the organist always wore the exact same shoes—no matter what color her dress was. They were flat, black Mary Janes, which were not unlike my own Sunday shoes then, except hers had paper-thin soles. They were not pretty shoes; in fact they were rather ugly. But to me they were like keys to the magic kingdom, and I wanted a pair of my own.

There was only one tiny obstacle. I was only five, too old for nursery, but too young for music lessons. So dreaming about it was the extent of my music career at that point. Nevertheless, I continued to watch and wait. Realizing my interest (perhaps the fact that I talked of little else had something to do with it), my parents (in the guise of Santa Claus) brought me a tiny little electric chord organ for Christmas that year, and it made me want to play a real organ even more.

I began with piano lessons at the age of ten. Why ten? Because, back in the dark ages when I was growing up, music teachers across America decided that until you were at least ten, you were not mature or serious enough to take piano lessons. I have marveled at that for years. Budding ballerinas and tiny toe-tappers were (and are) encouraged to begin taking dance lessons as soon as they could walk, but, back then, novice pianists had to be ten. So the wait began. And it went on. And on. And *on*. Even then, I was a tad impatient, but I was determined too. So I passed the years between five and ten pretending to play Beethoven on my electric chord organ, wearing my make-believe music-making Mary Janes, and longing for the day when I could take lessons, wear real organist's shoes, and play on an adult-sized musical instrument.

When I finally arrived at the milestone birthday, I didn't get the shoes, but I did get the music lessons. Mom and Dad decided that they would rent a piano to be sure I really was serious about music before committing to buying one. As the months passed, and my faithful promise to practice, practice, practice was kept, Mom bought me a piano with money she had received from her father as a gift. What a sacrifice! Of course, as a child, I had no idea she had done this, and when I found out years later, it overwhelmed me to know that she spent her gift money on a piano for her little girl. But that is what mothers do daily; they sacrifice to make dreams come true for their children. And my mother's sacrifice was not in vain. I was in love with music and still am.

A quote I read once on an antique piece of needlework has stayed with me ever since. It was attributed to Johann Sebastian Bach: "Music hath no purpose other than the glorification of God and the recreation of the soul." Even as a young child, long before I had ever heard those words or could even have understood them, music was my muse, and still is; it is the greatest thread that runs through my inner spirit and creative soul. In my lifetime, I have produced and created two piano and orchestral CDs, one as a gift for my son Eric and his wife Katie at their wedding, and a second disc of Christmas music that was sold and distributed nationally. I served as the staff organist for my church until I was 50 years old, and I have played for than 300 weddings and as many funerals. But before I was able to accomplish any of that, I had to master the basics. And in doing so, I learned an important lesson: Life isn't a do-over, but it *is* a start-over.

Mrs. Taft was my first music teacher. She lived in an old dark house equipped with a converted piano studio that had once been her living room. In it, she kept statues of all the great composers (though I didn't know who they were at the time) and pile upon pile of sheet music and books. She had two pianos: the grand she played, and a small spinet perfect for tiny hands like mine. Mrs. Taft also had two pairs of glasses. One was for every day, but the other gave her eagle-sharp vision, so powerful that she could sit at her piano and see the pages of even my music perfectly. She was well on in years and wore her hair in a neat little bun in the back with never a stray hair out of place. She was equally meticulous in her teaching methods, and at the ripe old age of ten, I had met my match. What I didn't learn, until much later—and not without a little pain— was that Mrs. Taft may have *looked* sweet and grandmotherly, but she was no push-over.

> We shall walk in velvet shoes, wherever we go.
> —Elinor Wylie

I was an eager student, but impatient. I loved the playing, but I was less enthusiastic about the slow and steady, step-by-step discipline of the learning process. I had grand visions of myself performing at Carnegie Hall to throngs of adoring music-lovers; the tedium of practicing scales and learning pieces note by note made me squirm. Music came very naturally to me, so I thought I could just bypass the basics and get on with it!

My own grandmother was a musician, one of such abundant natural ability that she could play the organ and piano by memory, or what musicians call "by ear." That is to say she could hear a piece played one time, then sit down and play it back note for note.

Mrs. Taft was also a wonderful pianist and a gifted teacher. I realized very quickly after beginning lessons with her that, like my grandmother, I could usually parrot it right back once I heard something played. My ability was buffeted by Mrs. Taft's use of the *John Thompson's Teaching Little Fingers to Play* books, that gave you a picture of your hand position, numbered the notes, and sent you on your way to playing success. This enabled me to, at a glance, learn the song I was assigned. And to further promote my rapid playing ability and my status as her star pupil, I always asked Mrs. Taft to *play* the piece she was assigning to me. What she didn't know was that after I heard her go over it once, I memorized the hand positions and numbers pictured in John Thompson's book. I could usually play every piece perfectly without a lot of practice and without ever learning to read the notes on the pages of music.

Many months rolled past, and Mrs. Taft marveled at my success as a student. In fact, I was going through her piano books like water—I could play just about anything in them. Mrs. Taft worked on a system of chits and rewards, the prize being gold foil stars that she stuck in the pages of each piece a student played from memory. Once you had earned enough stars and mastered ten songs, you could cash in the stars for a little marble statue. My collection of stars and statues grew exponentially.

One of the things no one had told me about was that my illustrious career as a concert pianist and organist was going to require me to perform for the public in recitals. I had never in my dreams considered *that*. And as if to pour salt on the wound, Mrs. Taft informed me that, as a matter of decorum, I had to *curtsy* prior to being seated on the bench and playing for my enchanted audience. I was in total rebellion. Curtsy? Not me. Who had started that little ritual anyway, I wondered, this curtsying before playing? I learned to curtsy, albeit a very abbreviated version, and my first recital came and went—another hurdle on the way to realizing my dream.

I remember it was a cool autumn day when I walked up to Mrs. Taft's house on Primm Lane for my weekly lesson.

I had memorized another piece or two and played them to her satisfaction, and she said to me the words I had waited to hear since I was five. "I think you are ready to play hymns from the church hymnal." I had arrived. This was it. My dream had come true. The hymnal placed on my music rack was open to my favorite hymn. The elation fluttering in my chest turned into a tickle of disbelief, which rapidly gave way to a shallow sense of dread. Where were the pictures, like the ones in John Thompson's book? Faced with no other option, I turned to my teacher and asked the earth-shaking question: Where were the *numbers*? Pale is the only word that comes to mind when trying to describe our faces as we both sat in her little piano studio staring at each other, she expecting me to play, me hoping she would quit kidding around.

"Numbers? What numbers?" she said in total bewilderment, clutching her collar bone. Sensing that my season as a piano prodigy was just about over, I explained to Mrs. Taft that I had been playing by numbers (much like paint by number) and that once I heard her play a song, I never had to bother with reading the music or learning to count the correct time. Reading those bars and spaces of a music staff was not even in my thought process, much less part of my learning experience. I had sidestepped the reading music part of the learning process, which was the core of playing the piano, and Mrs. Taft wasn't going to let me get away with it.

At the age of 10, I discovered that dreams may come true, but they take work; success never happens overnight. You know, I love movies; in fact, *The Sound of Music* was one of the first movies I ever remember seeing as a child, and I was (and still am) just swept away by every scene, every song, every sweet sentiment of that time-

> It is the flagrant lack of practicality that makes high-heeled shoes so fascinating.
> —Stephen Daylcy

less picture. But think for a moment how much is compressed into a mere 174 minutes: Maria leaves her life in the convent as a postulant, becomes a governess to seven unhappy children, wins them over, falls in love with their father, Captain Von Trapp, marries him, and flees the encroaching German army with her new family in tow. That's a heck of lot to happen in just under three hours! But that's what little girls grow up on—fairy tales and make-believe, Hollywood magic that give us a beginning, a middle, and an end in only a few hours.

Life, it turns out, is very different; it takes hard work and perseverance. Slow and steady wins the race.

I have taken that lesson with me through my own life. Just
like practicing the piano everyday was a discipline for learning music, practicing "forward thinking" has been a discipline
I have acquired as an adult. I believe that our minds and
thoughts can take us any direction at any time and our past
experiences will often hold us hostage to hurts, disappoint-
ments, failures, bad choices, sadness and regrets if we don't
learn to check those thoughts. Part of persevering and self-
discipline is learning to not only stay in the moment as you
work toward a goal, but also to shed baggage as you go. By
training yourself to think forward, you can keep your
thoughts centered on the here and now, while keeping the
prize—tomorrow's results of today's actions—firmly within
your sights.

I am today a product of my life to this point, both the
good and the bad. For many women, midlife is time to drop
the baggage and move forward. I have acquired plenty of
baggage in my time, from the ups and downs of my personal
life to building my company, selling it, and buying it back
again. Forward thinking is sometimes very hard to do, but
focusing our thoughts on the positive *must* be learned and
practiced until it becomes a habit, a way of life. I choose to
think forward and dream, learning from my past instead of
drowning in it, and letting it serve as a guide for me in making decisions today. I choose to be happy, to love life and

find humor in all things as I walk through life, and that lesson came early as I sat in Mrs. Taft's house on Primm Lane,
when the words "starting over from scratch" took on a new
meaning for me. Instead of being paralyzed by fear and giving up, I stopped where I was and started over from the
beginning. Easier than it sounds, it turns out.

Sweet little Mrs. Taft made me start over all right, this
time without numbers, sans pictures, and her own piano sat
silent. Not only did I feel like a felon, but recovery was not
going to be a cakewalk! After several months of learning the
mechanics of reading music and being disciplined enough to
work at the techniques of music, I got it. But it was not easy.
I learned the importance of daily discipline, of appreciating
method, and putting those lessons into practice. Oh, I
rebelled of course. Discipline for me meant staying between
white lines that someone else had drawn in order to accomplish *my* goal. I didn't like to be disciplined; I still don't. It
goes against my natural bent, my love of being spontaneous
in the current place I find myself and changing on a whim
if I want to change. But I learned that dreams take drive. If
you want to reach a goal, discipline is part of the process,
and because I still had my sights set on those organist's shoes
and all the beautiful music I could make wearing them, I
hung in there, and I left my previous missteps behind as I
moved forward.

I didn't get those shoes for almost another decade, not until
I was in college. I had been the church pianist for several

years when our organist moved away, leaving one lonely bench and one patient church. Our minister of music asked me if I would learn to play the organ. I flashed back to my early days in "big church," thought about those shoes, and responded, "Of course." He explained that it would be temporary until a suitable organist could be retained for the position.

More than 25 years later, I was still on the bench in the same pair of black leather shoes, playing for church services, weddings, funerals and all the life-altering events that seem to take place in church and which require a beautiful soundtrack. Today, when I think of magic shoes, I think of my organist's shoes. Though they are the ugliest pair I own, I love them because they symbolize for me one of the most soul-satisfying parts of my life—music—and also the idea that though there is no easy way of getting what you want, you *can* get it anytime you are ready. No matter what your circumstances or dreams, whatever it is you want to be or become, start right now. Not tomorrow. Today. Let go of past mistakes and insecurities, put one foot in front of the other, and just get going. Getting there will take time and effort, of that there is no doubt, but moving forward rather than standing still or looking behind is the key to success, as is faith.

Remember Dorothy's fabulous, red sequined shoes from *The Wizard of Oz*, and how they sparkled with every step she took? Those shoes were indeed magic, but not in the way the mean old Wicked Witch of the West thought. Dorothy faithfully followed the yellow brick road all the way to Oz in search of the wizard to help her get home, only to discover that what she really needed to make her wish come true had been in her heart the whole time. The wizard was a fake, and the shoes didn't hold any supernatural powers. But they *did* take her where she wanted to go—all the way back home to Kansas. We're all the same as little Dorothy Gale. Our hearts' desire is within reach if we're just willing to keep moving forward with courage and conviction. Faith, and learning to stay in the moment, not only moves mountains, it can help you traverse them too. Just be sure you choose the right shoes for the journey. You never know what discoveries you might make along the way!

DOROTHY'S RUBY SLIPPERS

The late Salvatore Ferragamo got his start as a shoemaker early in life; he made his first pair of lady's shoes at age 9 for his sister to wear to her communion. After he was established in his trade, the celebrated Italian "Shoemaker to the Stars," became so renowned that his designs were sought after by everyone from Eva Peron to Marilyn Monroe. But his most famous design is perhaps his least credited: the ruby-red, glittering pumps worn by Judy Garland as Dorothy in the 1939 classic, *The Wizard of Oz*.

Interestingly, the shoes were silver in the best-selling book on which the film was based, but the film's screenwriter felt silver would not catch the eye as much on screen as red, so he changed it. Costume designers at MGM made six pairs of the sequined slippers for filming, four of which survived. One pair is displayed at the Smithsonian, another pair at Disney MGM studio, and a third pair sold at a Christie's auction in 2000 for $666,000. Where the fourth pair can be found is anybody's guess. They were stolen in 2005 while on loan to the Judy Garland Museum in Minnesota and have never been recovered. They were insured for one million dollars.

CHAPTeR

4

Shoes to Fill

My Aunt Lorene Norton was one of the most put-together women I have ever known, and one of the first women, besides my mother, who really made an impression on me as a young girl. How I wanted to follow in her footsteps! She dated my dad's younger brother, Jack; in fact, they dated for six years before they married and she "officially" became my aunt. She worked for the phone company both before and after the engagement, which was unheard of for a Southern lady (or really any lady) at that time, and Aunt Lorene was as unflappable as she was fashionable.

Through my little girl's eyes, she seemed the epitome of glamour and self-confidence. Aunt Lorene was a self-made

39

woman who worked in a man's world, but she was all woman, the very picture of Southern belle femininity in her stylish dresses, tailored suits, and gorgeous sweater sets. She was always groomed to exquisite perfection, and I remember she had a narrow, sleek foot that looked fabulous in heels, and she had the most beautiful collection of classic, stylish shoes that never seemed to age or go out of style.

While they were still dating and after they married, Aunt Lorene and Uncle Jack frequently went to my grandmother's home on weekends; that's when she and I would get the chance to visit. She was the kind of woman Mary Tyler Moore made famous a couple of decades later in the seventies—

> It is all very well for so-called sensible people to recommend flat heels and short skirts, but most of us prefer not to be so sensible.
> —Anna Held

single, strong-minded, professional, capable, yet still beautiful and soft around the edges. She always looked perfect, right down to coordinating her lipstick and nail polish to match her flawless outfits. Now, Southern women are practically required to a have a signature color when it comes to lipstick and nail polish, and Lorene's was Mocha Polka by Revlon, but if she chose to wear, say, a tangerine suit, she made sure her lips and nails matched! She always dressed in ensembles, never trendy separates, and what she couldn't afford to buy, she sewed or embellished for herself because she wanted to always have pretty clothes to wear to work. I remember she had an especially stunning royal blue sweater set that she had made even more gorgeous by adding a rabbit fur collar beaded with tiny pearls—it was divine, and the perfect example of how Aunt Lorene could take something ordinary and nice and make it into a one-of-kind piece using her imagination, her skill, and only a little bit of money. Southern women love to look pretty, we're famous for that, but we're also taught to make do with what we've got. Aunt Lorene exemplified that, as did my mother.

My mother began teaching me early on how to become a woman. She was and still is the most beautiful woman in the world, and like my Aunt Lorene, she has always been, for me, the epitome of style. There is nothing that Mom won't try, and she usually masters whatever she attempts. She has sparkling blue eyes, and even today, at eighty-two years old, she can still cause more mischief than any person you would hope to meet

When Mom was a young bride, Dad was overseas in the Navy. While he was away, she lived at home with her parents on a farm in North Alabama, and her brothers gave her bus money to go to work in town as an executive assistant. They wanted her to buy pretty clothes and shoes with the money she earned, and she did! But she was creative too. She was, and remains, a master seamstress and can copy any outfit she sees! She is also a gifted embellisher. She could take a plain purse or shoes and make them special by adding special little touches and flourishes. She was a devoted mother, wife, and homemaker, but she was a fashion plate too!

I remember her wearing exquisitely cut suits that she made herself, and she also made clothes for me, my sister Janice, and even my brother Keith. In the seventies, Mom, Janice and I would glue ourselves every Friday night to the television to watch *Dallas*. Janice was Pam Ewing and I was Sue Ellen, and even though we didn't have their million dollar budgets for clothes, we didn't need them. We had Mom. She could look at their outfits on the show and then copy them to perfection. It was wonderful!

She always told me that it is better to have a few truly fabulous outfits than a closet filled with junk. She is right about that. One basic suit can be anything you need with brooches, scarves, or blouses. If, for instance, you wear a plain and simple peep-toe slingback with a black suit, you'll fit into any board room or office. Change into red stilettos, though, and you're ready for a night out on the town. She also taught me that even the smallest details deserved attention. One of my fondest memories of my mother and other women from her era is the effort they put into getting the seams straight in their stockings! To get them just right, a woman had to hook each stocking to a garter belt and keep adjusting until the seam was as straight as an arrow, and then constantly check one's posterior view in a mirror to make sure they stayed that way! Mom looked great in them, and she always completed the look in classic heels. She has always insisted that heels make your legs look fabulous, even if you don't have great legs!

One of Mom's icons of style (and my own) was, of course, Jackie Kennedy. The young but regal First Lady in kitten heels was a fashion phenomenon whose classic separates came together for a perfected whole, and every button, every belt, every pillbox hat she wore became all the rage the second she was photographed in it. My mother too fell under the First Lady's fashionable spell. Mom filled her own closet with hats; boxy little suits; simple, streamlined frocks that she dressed up with simple accessories; and cocktail-length evening gowns that transformed her from a mother and wife to a chic lady when she wore them. And like Jackie Kennedy, she always took pains to complete the picture of finery with the perfect pair of shoes.

One pair stands out in my memory—they were turquoise satin evening shoes that even had a little clutch evening bag dyed to match. Mother always wore them with a gorgeous duchess satin dress in the same vibrant shade. She looked stunning each time she wore that ensemble, like a princess, and putting it on meant that a grand occasion of some sort was on the horizon. When I saw her in it, I would say in my stage whisper voice, with stars in my eyes, "You look *beautiful!*" as her radiance seemed to fill the room. I could close my

 eyes and envision Mom and Dad dancing together cheek to cheek, with her full skirt whirling around and those fabulous pointed-toe aquamarine shoes gliding across the floor, looking for all the world like Cinderella in the arms of her Prince Charming, but prettier.

When she wasn't wearing them, Mother packed those lovely pumps away in the box they came in, each stiletto individually and carefully wrapped in protective layers of tissue. On rainy days, or sometimes "just because," my sister Janice and I would plead with Mom to unpack those amazing shoes and let us play dress-up. She would succumb to our pleas and stand guard nearby as my little sister and I would slip our tiny feet into them and then wobble clumsily around her room. We must have looked like we were trying to walk on stilts, but we felt like we were walking on air. In a flash, we were three inches taller; we became sophisticates with the same bird's-eye view of the world our beautiful mother enjoyed. Or so we pretended. We would paint ourselves in Mother's lipstick, dust on layers of chalky powder, adorn ourselves in every bead or bangle of hers we could put on, then make believe we were on our way to a ball, assuring ourselves that life would be like that someday when we were all grown up: total sophistication and womanhood in all its glory!

In reality, of course, we were more like Lucy and Ethel than Cinderella and the Fairy Godmother. When we took our first steps in Mother's evening shoes, we came close to breaking our necks. It was possible that the heel would snap in two and we just might tumble right down the stairs, but putting on those shoes was a risk we were willing to take for the privilege of dressing and feeling like a woman. Ever the Little Miss Priss, my sister Janice, who was three years younger than me, perfected walking in Mom's oversize heels long before I did, but I was determined. Arms akimbo to keep my balance, I would tentatively place one foot in front of the other, rocking to and fro as I went. But with each attempt, the walk became easier. And as we became steadier on our feet, it made us sad to return to our flat black velvet Mary Janes after that lofty experience.

Looking around my home today, the tell-tale imprint of my mother's sure touch is everywhere: in the needlework samplers that she taught me to appreciate, in the paintings she created with her own brush and palette, and in the ivy-patterned dinnerware from my childhood that she passed along to me as an early family heirloom. She's in my shoe closet too! I own a pair of satin pumps that, while not an exact replica of Mother's perfect pair, are almost as pretty. And my mother's penchant for clean, elegant, classic styles is there too, as well as her fondness for color, both reflected in the staggering array of kitten and stiletto heels I have accrued over the years.

Perhaps more than anyone, my mother helped me define and determine my worth as a woman, as a *lady*, and I cherish her. She is my greatest cheerleader, my kindest critic, my dearest comforter, and my greatest teacher. And while she certainly tops the list of women whom I revere and who have influenced and helped shape me, she is not alone in that canon. From my late Aunt Lorene to my little sister Janice to my oldest and dearest friend Barbara, I have learned something valuable from all the women in my life. From Aunt Lorene, I learned that being single, smart, ambitious, and strong-minded was as much a part of being a woman as the shoes we wear; from my sister Janice I have received the gift of endless laughter and the courage to occasionally wear *outrageously* showy shoes just for fun; and from Barbara, I have learned, among other things, the importance of maintaining a ladylike but unflappable dignity, even in the face of life's most painful and humbling moments.

It is a privilege to have these and other wonderful women in my life. All of them have fearlessly developed their own personal style and stuck with it. They have learned from their individual experiences and generously shared the insights they have gained along the way with other women. Through their reflections, I have been able to hold them up to myself like a mirror so I can get a clearer picture of who I am and who I *could* be. As women, I believe it is imperative that we learn from each other and nurture each other—I have based my entire career, and this book, on that very notion. Read my magazines and you'll learn not only about women's interests, but about our inner and outer lives as well. I believe that, as women, we are constantly evolving, and I also believe that my female friends, peers, and loved ones are a lot like my shoes. Each one is precious and pretty in some special way; each one is perfect for a specific occasion; and without them, my closet, and my life, would be empty.

KiTTeN HeeLS

When a very young, very demure Jacqueline Kennedy ascended to the White House, she immediately captured the country's imagination as a quintessential lady with a fashion sense that remains unsurpassed by her successors. She exuded youthful sophistication, wearing immaculately tailored, streamlined designer dresses and suits, glittering but simple evening gowns, and accessorizing each ensemble to perfection with modest jewelry, handbags, and pretty (albeit size 10) shoes.

Mrs. Kennedy's official wardrobe designer was Oleg Cassini, who referred to his most famous client as a "geometrical goddess." He coordinated every element of her Camelot wardrobe, from her day and evening wear to her hats and to her shoes. In footwear, the First Lady tended toward a somewhat conservative, ultra-feminine look. She favored flats and ladylike kitten

heels that matched and complimented her gorgeous garments and
which were as simple, elegant, and timeless as the legendary
triple-strand pearls she wore so frequently and with such élan.
Her wardrobe was a constant source of clamor and discourse,
inciting praise as well as a few stinging barbs from pundits who
felt she spent an inordinate amount of money on clothing. The
fashionable First Lady took it all in stride, however, reacting
publicly with little more than a slight sense of bemusement:
"All the talk over what I wear and how I fix my hair has amused
and puzzled me . . . What does my hairdo have to do with my
husband's ability to be President?"

CHAPTER 5

Shoes in Training

When I try to recall the morning of December 25, 1958, I hear the hollow padding of six pint-size feet (me, my brother Keith, and my baby sister Janice) running down the hallway and into the living room to see what Santa had left for us under the Christmas tree. We had taken great pains, you see, to mind our Ps and Qs, especially as December drew nigh, and I remember how confident I felt that the always jolly and ever-discerning Saint Nick had added me to his "good list" and would reward me in due measure. If I close my eyes, I can still smell the clean, wintry fragrance of the cedar tree and, in my mind's eye, I can see as plain as day the cantina-style lights glowing against the green of the branches and boughs in Crayola shades of red and blue and yellow, bouncing off the shiny printed paper of the packages that lay beneath. And I remember exactly how I felt when I opened my favorite present that year. In fact, all the other gifts from Santa have faded into fuzzy memories at best, but my first pair of high heels? Those I remember.

> The shoe that fits one person pinches another.
> —Carl Jung

They were the most beautiful things I had ever seen; they were those plastic high heels that came in a dress-up kit for little women in training. I know you remember them too! Every little girl in America got that present at some point, at Christmas or for a birthday, perhaps. Oh, remember? They were always pink or silver, spiky little mules with elastic bands to hold them on your feet, and little princesses in waiting, prom queens in the making, movie star hopefuls, and future brides all loved them. They always came packaged with a matching tiara and a set of Pop Beads in a coordinating color. For those of you who are clueless to the magic of Pop Beads, they are the most fabulous piece of costume jewelry ever invented. Still made today, Pop Beads (also called Snap Beads) are strands of plastic pearl-shaped beads that snap together and snap apart so that you can change the length at will, or even make a necklace and matching bracelet. Wouldn't it be great if you could do that today with real pearls? The beads, the bejeweled tiara, and those wonderful plastic shoes were the perfect ensemble for a young girl like me, who was already dreaming of her future, one in which I would be swept off my feet in my queen's crown, my Pop Beads, and the most glamorous shoes ever designed.

And how *deliciously* deceptive those heels were! They looked so innocent and pretty in the package, but they were misery to wear. I'm not sure which suffered more that Christmas, my dignity or my ankles, because I must have fallen a thousand times trying to walk in them. In reality, they couldn't have been more than an inch or two high, but I felt like I was standing on skyscrapers. Up I'd stand and down I'd go, arms flapping wildly like nothing so much as a duck trying to take flight from the water's surface. I'd tell you about the bruises I got in *certain places*, but polite Southern ladies don't talk about such things in mixed company. Despite the ups and downs, I kept at it. Bruised ego and other, er, parts notwithstanding, I wanted for all the world to strut around in those shoes like a proper young lady. Teetering around two inches off the ground, I got a glimpse of what lay ahead for me as a young woman, and frankly, I wasn't exactly over the moon about it. Part of me, the bruised part of me, thought "if this is being a girl, I'm out!"

Those shoes had *looked* so wonderful, but wearing them? That was a different matter. But as women learn, even at the most tender of ages, I discovered that once you step into certain shoes, they're yours and there's no turning back.

Now, my baby sister Janice had her own pair of "practice heels" and, in true fashion, she took to them like she'd been born in them. But Janice is more of a "pink" girl, while I'm more of a "red" girl. Pink girls like ribbons and bows and lacy dresses; red girls love tailored dresses, sleek lines, and sometimes being a tomboy. But we share a common ground; we are like salt and pepper. Pink is the soft, vulnerable side of red and red is the adventurous, daring side of pink, and as I grow older, I'm discovering more of my pink side as I go. But when I was stumbling around in those princess heels as a young girl, I wasn't strutting around like I owned the world. I was struggling just to walk across the room! I wanted to take them off, sling them aside, put on my tennis shoes, and go play baseball with the boys.

But just as my need and love for shoes is innate, so then was my courage and my willingness to consider or at least *pretend* to be a little less "red" and a little more "pink." I decided I had better embrace femininity, because what choice did I have really? I can tell you that the day I asked for a tube of lipstick instead of a football, my mother was overjoyed. That was in my junior high years, and being feminine started to seem more attractive and feel more natural, which, though exciting, also took a little extra courage on my part. Like

every "tween," all I *really* wanted was to blend into the wall-
paper as I struggled with the inevitable physical and emotional changes that come with maturing. But I stood head and
shoulders over the petite little Barbie doll girls in my class, so
fading into the background was impossible. I decided to just
go ahead and jump in feet first. I told my mother I thought it
was time for my first pair of grown-up heels, and once I
warmed up to the idea, I started to feel flutters of excitement
about trying them out and showing them off.

I remember them well; they were navy blue pumps with
two-inch heels, and I got them just in time for the junior high
school Christmas concert, a big annual to-do at my school,
Gresham Junior High, held each holiday season in the school
gym and performed by the concert choir. I was to accompany
the singers on piano, and I couldn't wait to debut my new
grown up heels in front of the whole school. Of course, I
would have to find them first. A friend from church, Lynne
Jackson, had found her first heels at Baker Shoes, a fashionable local shoe store, and had turned up with them at church
the previous Sunday. Lynne and I did not go to the same
school, so I figured buying a pair exactly like hers would work
for me. Mom took me to the store and out I came with a navy

blue pair just like the ones I had so admired on
Lynne's feet during Sunday school.

That unopened box sat in my bed-
room and seemed to whisper my
name, and besides, practice makes

perfect, so I thought I had better try them out at home before stepping out in them in public. My first few steps were wobbly and painful! I remember the feeling of standing up in them for the first time, taking a few steps, and wondering if I would ever walk straight again. I practiced all night, fumbling around the house until I thought I had the hang of it! I got up the next morning with a spring in my step. Suddenly, I couldn't *wait* to put on those shoes. This was a true rite of passage—a day where I would finally leave pin curls and pinafores behind and cross over into glamour and sophistication.

I could hardly wait to get to school, knowing that I would be noticed by all, especially the guys. And to top it off, I would also be wearing honest-to-Pete real pantyhose in a beautiful taupe color! (Though bare legs may be the fashion today, a young Southern lady in my day would *never* have worn proper heels without hose! She would have been ostracized by her peers and shamed by her mother, who would have cried and cried over a daughter who didn't even know to wear pantyhose. That was serious stuff.) Since I was the pianist, all I had to do was make it to the bench and sit down. A perfect setting and a perfect plan.

Being fourteen years old and attempting this glamour move was a disaster. Oh, I got noticed by every guy in the gym, all right. Specifically, the entire basketball team. When I glided (in my mind I was definitely gliding) across the gym, all the players screamed at me to get off the newly varnished gym floor in those clickety-clack shoes! Yikes! This was hardly the reception I had dreamed of, and to make it worse, I could barely walk in my still not-broken-in heels, so there was no getting off the floor, much less "right now," as the rather vocal young men on the basketball team were so vehemently demanding. The clicking sound of those shoes still echoes in my mind today like a slow motion instant replay. I did the only thing I could think to do. I held my chin up, kept my gaze forward, and kept on walking!

Oh, I wanted to run away, but there was no way around it—any of it. No matter what, I wasn't going to be able to escape being the tallest girl in class, I wasn't going to get around walking across that floor, and I was going to, like it or not, finish in the shoes I started out in. It was like my mother always told me: "If you're going to get blamed for it, do it." My daughter-in-law Katie has another saying I like, and one that also applied to that excruciating walk in those brand-new high heels: "It's go big or go home." Because it's in my nature as a "red" girl, I went for it. I went big, and strutted my way across that gym floor like there was no tomorrow.

That next Sunday, when the second wearing of the shoes was inevitable, I couldn't wait to show off my new shoes to Lynne at church. There she was, all decked out in her own pair of navy blue heels, and I made a beeline to her pew to sit beside her. To my utter amazement, her heels were a full one inch shorter than mine! No wonder she moved with grace and ease—she could actually walk in *hers*!

"Keeping up with the Joneses" is a phrase that has been used to death in the South. Actually, I am not about keeping up with anyone; I am about playing to win, and I always have been. I was totally undone over the fact that Lynne had scooped me with the first pair of real heels, and even more irritated that she had the good sense to get heels tall enough to be considered a lady's heel but still short enough to enjoy and move around in with ease. But the two-inchers were mine, and I had to wear them and make the best of it (shall we say, living with my mistake). Don't you just hate that—living with something that can't be undone? I couldn't ask my parents to pay for another expensive pair of heels until those were worn out. And to make matters worse, since I was the tallest girl in my class, when I wore them, I *really* towered above most everyone. What was I thinking? I have been confronted with this many times in life. We've all bitten off more than we can chew at some point, and I am no exception.

> Remember, Ginger Rogers did everything that Fred Astaire did, but she did it backward and in high heels.
> —Faith Whittlesey

It's funny. Today, whether I'm trying on and rejecting sky-high heels at Macy's or just playing dress-up in my own shoe closet, I can't help but remember that first little plastic pair of shoes from so many Christmases ago. Our first play shoes, I think, are more than just toys given to coddle our little-girl longing to play dress-up. Even though we may not know it at the time, they are about rehearsing for our future. We learn that to walk in those shoes, you have to take it one baby step at a time, and before you know it, you are steady on your feet and walking around in those shoes like you were born in them; they even start to feel good. But it takes patience and courage to take it one step at a time as you learn. What's more, the slower you move, the more you might take in along the way, some of it good, and inevitably, some of it will be bad too. Just like learning to walk in those little princess heels, and later on in the real thing, as women, sometimes we have to just keep moving no matter how great the obstacles we face and no matter how many times we stumble and trip over the landscape, or even our own feet. The trick is to just keep moving and forging ahead with courage, bravado, and *style*. My motto today is "red lipstick, high heels, and big hair." Go big or go home? I'll go big, thanks, every time. And I'll do it in heels.

FiT FOR A QUeeN

On display at the Reading Museum in England is a pair of rare and beautifully restored heels known as "Queen Elizabeth's Slippers." The whimsical shoes are covered in red, green, and blue silk with pomegranate and leaf motifs, and each slipper is fitted with a wooden clog and heel. By 2006, experts had discarded the notion that the shoes did indeed belong to the seventeenth-century queen, but they do give the curious a vivid example of the style of footwear the monarch fancied.

Though she was not the male heir her father Henry VIII had so hoped for, Queen Elizabeth I was one of England's greatest and strongest rulers—and definitely one of its better dressed. The Virgin Queen understood all too well what power a woman's appearance could give her, and she took care with every detail from head to toe, using her wardrobe as one of her most potent political weapons. And because apparel was a primary indicator of status in the Elizabethan era, she demanded that her jewel-encrusted, embroidered gowns be without rival, and was known to upbraid ladies-in-waiting whose finery dared to compete with her own. On her head she wore a crown, and her feet were equally adorned with royal majesty.

The fashion-conscious queen always presented herself in public and in portraits wearing beautiful shoes, many of which only peeked out from beneath her splendid gowns. Her meticulously

kept wardrobe records indicate Queen
Elizabeth I, an avid horse rider, owned a
pair or two of boots known as buskins, but
she was particularly fond of velvet flats
and pantobles, slippers made with
deep cork sole and thick, elevated heel. These were custom-
made (often to match a specific
outfit) from leather, velvet,
satin, and silk, and according
to records, embellished with
embroidery, precious gems, and

gold and silver lace. A wardrobe account dating circa 1600 reports
the queen had amassed, among other items, 99 robes, 102 French
gowns, 100 loose gowns, 125 petticoats, 96 cloaks, 27 fans, and
9 pairs of pantobles.

Popular across Europe, pantobles were also called "chopines,"
and they were typically made of either wood or cork. The stilt-like
shoes sported heels as high as 20 or more inches, and were
designed to save a lady's dress hem from dragging through the
muck of muddy city streets. The height of the shoe was also an
indicator of social standing; the higher the heel the greater the
status of the woman wearing it. The women who wore the often
unwieldy chopines frequently employed either servants or canes to
help maintain balance as they struggled to walk in them.

CHAPTER

6

Playing to Win

For some women, competition can be a dirty word. That can be especially true for Southern women, where qualities such as graciousness, courtesy, and hospitality are praised—and rightly so—as sought-after feminine virtues. In that context, the word "competitive" can conjure up ugly images of wanting to win at any cost. But when I compete in business, and even in my personal life, the object is to get there first and grab the best seat! I compete for the joy of it, for the exhilarating fun of it, and other women have been some of my greatest mentors in that arena.

I wish that you could know my friend Joan Chamblee to fully appreciate what I like to think of as The Striped Suede Shoes Saga of 1993. Joan is sister-in-law to Charles Chamblee, one of my dearest friends and professional mentors at Ernst & Young, the first company I worked for as a young accountant, but our friendship goes back farther than my career as a CPA and our bond is much deeper. Joan and I were old maids together, you see. Now for those of you who didn't come of age in the seventies in the South, what that means is this: We were the only two single women in our church over the age of twenty-two. Trust me, our mothers were getting nervous.

Joan and I hated going to bridal teas and showers because we knew that, inevitably, someone would ask: "When is it your turn?" We made a pact that we would never, *ever* go to a wedding-related event of any sort unless we went together. We'd show up and when the questions started flying from the hostesses and curious guests, Joan and I would slip into our Mary Richards and Rhoda Morgenstern routine and coyly divert the questions. "Our turn for what?" we'd ask, eyelashes batting. It worked beautifully, and Joan and I really were like our TV counterparts from *The Mary Tyler Moore Show*: I was spunky, career-minded, and turning the world on with my smile (or at least trying to), while Joan was colorful and trendy and free-spirited. Like Rhoda, she is all bling and no beige; in fact, Joan is the only woman I know who actually accessorizes her *swimsuits* with matching earrings.

During our college years and into adulthood, our weekends were spent gabbing, gossiping, and treasure hunting for bargains together, trying to find the greatest deals in the world—and beat each other to the cash register. By the time the two of us were in our midtwenties, two men had come along and married us, getting us safely off the proverbial streets, or so our grateful mothers said at the time. Our twosome became a foursome, and soon expanded with children on both sides; I had twin boys and she had twins too—a daughter and son. A few years later she had another daughter to get ahead of me again!

Now, as much as we have always loved and supported each other, sharing some of the greatest milestones of our lives from marriage to children, there has always been a distinct spirit of competition between us—especially in our long-standing, mutual quest for the latest fashions, the most gorgeous jewelry, and, of course, the very best bargain-priced shoes! I am sad to report that Joan is ahead right now—she recently received a five-carat diamond ring for her thirtieth wedding anniversary. She actually *named* her diamond "Gloria," short for "Gloria in Excelsis Deo." Her jeweler even knows the diamond has been named; I bet she has him keep a birth certificate on file. Don't worry that she'll beat me though. I will come up with something to stun her!

But back in the days when Joan and I could only dream of such jewels, when we were just starting out, she and her family moved to Atlanta when her husband, Gary, got transferred.

I cried. I pleaded. How could Mary and Rhoda split up, for heaven's sake? I was slightly consoled by the intriguing notion that not only could I visit fairly often, but the move *did* open up a world of shopping options that Joan and I didn't have in Birmingham. So visits to Atlanta always centered around our race to cover all the great shops in the metropolitan area. We were so rowdy, our kids would not shop with us, opting to hang out with their dads, who they mistakenly believed to be much cooler than we were. To this day, those kids don't know that we slyly planned it that way so they would go with their dads and leave us to shop in peace! We should have received Oscars for our award-winning performances.

Now, Joan is a woman who knows exactly what she wants and she doesn't mind asking for it—the kind of lady who never, ever orders off the menu, much to the frequent embarrassment of her children. She and I are so close we can finish each other's sentences, so when we got together and wanted a little "us" time away from the husbands and children, the Mary and Rhoda routine kicked right back in without missing a beat. Our theatrics were absolutely brazen! Her children and my sons would stand in mute horror while we playfully planned bra-shopping excursions or forgot to use our "inside voices" in stores when discussing our cleavage. That one *always* worked. We would get so tickled at each other; we would laugh until tears were rolling down our cheeks. Our poor kids would look like they wanted to just melt into the carpet, and they would *beg* us to let them hang

out with their fathers instead. We always
obliged.

The Saga of the Striped Suede
Shoes occurred during one of our
infamous Atlanta shopping sprees. I
vividly remember it; it was shortly
before my fortieth birthday. There was a
wonderful boutique in a shopping mall near
Joan's home, and the shoe selection was just beyond description. The shoes were very unique and very chic, like a pair of
Carrie Bradshaw's dream shoes on *Sex and the City*, and in the
window was a drop-dead gorgeous pair of black suede shoes
with multi-colored stripes! Now, anyone who knows me will
tell you I love patterned and textured shoes, and the more
eccentric, the better: tiger and zebra stripes, giraffe prints,
polka dots, suede with metal studs, two toned cap toe heels,
peau de soie, and satin in every color of the rainbow and
beyond!

When I was growing up, it was navy, black, white, brown,
and grey—those were your choices when it came to shoes—
so when footwear fashions began to include patterns, prints,
and multiple hues, I was overjoyed. I even have a spotted pair
of what have been referred to as my Cruella De Vil shoes.
Ha! I think every woman should receive such a compliment,
but even those little darlings were nothing in comparison to
the striped pair that dazzled me so in that store window,
beckoning me inside. I was in love and I didn't care what they

> I don't know who invented high heels, but all women owe him a lot.
> —Marilyn Monroe

cost. I would sell something if I had to in order to take those babies home with me. I floated in on air and asked for them in my size. I could hardly sit still while waiting for the clerk to bring the box out with those show-stoppers inside.

I carefully pulled back the tissue and there they were in all their perfect striped glory. Heaven! I slipped one on like Cinderella's slipper . . . except. No wait. It couldn't be. I wiggled my foot around inside and . . . too small. I was confused, bewildered, but the clerk, sensing her big fish of a sale was about to swim away from her, dashed to the back and brought out a matching pair, in the next largest size. Good thing, she told me, that was the only other pair in the store. But fate is a cruel mistress sometimes, and when I tried the second pair on, they wouldn't fit either. One pair was too big and the other was too small. Lord *help*, all of a sudden I became Goldilocks.

There is nothing more devastatingly torturous for a shoe fanatic like me than to be *between sizes*. Ordinarily I would buy the smaller size, stretch them out (wear 'em while you vacuum ladies; they'll fit in no time), and then debut them at church. But these hurt so badly, I knew there was no way they would ever fit, not even if I cleaned house for two days straight in them! And the other pair was so large I was walking out of them every time I took even a teeny little step. I just sat there in total shock. When Joan and I left the store, I turned back to look at them longingly one more time as we proceeded to head for greener shoe-shopping pastures. But all day long, I kept mentally comparing every pair I tried on to those striped suede shoes, and they all came up lacking. I was heartsick.

Several weeks passed and my birthday drew closer. Though I didn't know it, my family and friends had planned a wonderful surprise dinner for my birthday at The Summit Club, a fantastic private dining and social club in Birmingham. I was totally caught off guard and was thrilled to see so many friends there, many of whom I hadn't seen in years. All of a sudden the elevator doors opened and out stepped Joan and Gary. I was overwhelmed! The Rhoda to my Mary had driven all the way from Atlanta just to come to my party. And she looked beautiful too. She was wearing a stunning black column dress that fit her like a velvet glove, and then my eyes fell to her feet. The room seemed to go dim and I felt my face go numb as I tried to smile at her. She, on the other hand, was grinning like a Cheshire cat and her perfectly painted red lips made her smile that much brighter. She was wearing *my* shoes. The stripes seemed to glow like neon! Joan had me again.

> The red shoes, they are "follow me" shoes.
> —Christian Louboutin

I could hardly concentrate on dinner as I kept shooting my friend those "I'll get you" looks that I am famous for. Joan just kept tilting her head to the side and smiling, ignoring the sort-of playful daggers I was sending her with my eyes.

To this day, Joan has those shoes in her closet and reminds me of them every chance she gets. Our children even talk about the striped shoes and her scooping me with them. It has been fifteen years and I still remember it like it just happened yesterday. We can laugh about it now, though I have to confess, she laughs more than I do.

I am a naturally competitive person and I play to win. I love practical jokes, both playing them and having them played on me. I love a good laugh, but I also love the exhilaration of competition; it adds great spice to life! And when you compete, sometimes you're going to lose. Nobody but nobody bats a thousand. Just like Joan got me with those shoes and that diamond! I laugh inside at her ability to get the best of me from time to time. Competition when kept in check is a good thing. It keeps us on our toes. Competing can also make us face who we really are inside. In the book of Luke, there is a verse in chapter six that I love that tells us, "The good man brings good things out of the good stored up in his heart, and the evil man brings evil things out of the evil stored up in his heart. For out of the overflow of his heart his mouth speaks." To me, that's what competition does—it either brings out the best or the worst in people.

When I started working, I managed to land a job as a CPA in the Birmingham office of the prestigious firm Ernst & Young. There were good men there, but not all of them warmed up to the idea of having women as co-workers; it was tough sledding for young women then. Remember, this was the seventies, and women were just entering the workforce full-on, and there were plenty of men who didn't adjust so well to leaving a wife at home only to be greeted by a gaggle of women at the office. Of course, it had never dawned on me that I wasn't "supposed" to be there, at least not until I arrived.

On my first day, I walked in wearing a no-nonsense grey wool suit, two-inch black, all-business pumps, and a smile. One of the partners, Hilton Dean, handed me a briefcase, a key, and a book of policies, rules, procedures, and dress codes, which, by necessity, now also addressed acceptable business attire for women. To my dismay, these guidelines included shoe restrictions (simple, unadorned pumps were the standard). Hilton uttered exactly two words: "Follow them." I proceeded to explain to him that I would be fashionably inhibited under these new "parameters" and that I was exactly the right person to bring style to the table, as well as the skills required of an accountant. He laughed.

My next introduction was to Travis Kirkpatrick, the direct supervisor who had been assigned to me. He was even less open to my ideas on revolutionizing work fashions at Ernst & Young. Travis was a big, burly, barrel-chested man whose sheer physical presence could intimidate, an aura that was fueled by his sometimes gruff, always aggressive personality. I thought I would die on my first day when he took one look at me and spoke his first words as one colleague to another:

"Goddamned women should stay home, make babies, and bake bread." My response was brief, "Welcome to the firm." But inside, I was thinking, "Let the games begin. If this is how you want to play it, go ahead. You have just set the stage for what life is going to be like working with me!"

Now, I love the kind of friendly competition I had always enjoyed with Joan, and with other women. But men can be different. For me, it had always been about having fun. But this was a different arena, and so I either had to learn new rules and quickly, or make up new ones. I chose to meet all those men head-on, but on *my* terms, and my secret weapon was as simple as it was potent: Humor. Always leave them laughing was, and remains, my standard operating procedure, particularly in business. Humor not only relaxes people, it disarms them.

Moreover, few people can resist a good laugh—even old Kirkpatrick came around. Later that year, when Halloween rolled around, I taped a card to his door and ran like a rabbit! It read, "This Halloween, let's go as a horse. I'll go as the head and you go as yourself." I could hear Travis bellowing my name all the way down the hall, but he was laughing too. That cemented our life-long friendship. A few years later, when I had my sons, I sent him a photograph of us all with a single sentence: "Not only can I bake bread, but I can have babies two at a time."I had never forgotten what he said to me on that first nerve-wracking day as a young up-and-comer, and I didn't let him forget it either. I had the last word too—but I did it with humor.

I think that, just as men do, women begin competing very early and very naturally, but it's not always easy for us to do it gracefully. We're creatures of emotion, and all too often we are insecure. We aren't always trained, as little boys are, that you win some, you lose some, and when you dish it out, you have to be able to take it too, and no matter how it ends, you shake hands with your adversary when the game is finished. Most importantly, to become a truly great competitor, you must learn that your value as a person is not tied to the outcome. If you attach your self worth to always winning, you will never get there. The goal line will only keep moving, leaving you feeling inadequate. There is great rest in being yourself and knowing that God made you just as he wanted you to be in the first place, and that's what makes you a worthy opponent. You have to learn to compete for the sheer love of the game and the pleasure playing it can bring you, not because you think always winning and never losing will turn you into the person you wish you were.

> Shoes are the first adult machines we are given to master.
> —Nicholson Baker

I love to see women become secure in who they are and recognize that they are created as individuals, each one with special gifts and talents. Here's a secret: It takes years to come to this point and many experiences to teach us this valuable life lesson, but once you learn to become secure in your own skin, you can begin to play the game, whatever yours may be, with grace and style. And you can compete with the best of them and win every time—even when the outcome isn't in your favor. Now all that said, I have to admit, I hate to lose, and when I do, I never forget it. And if by chance, I should shuffle off this mortal coil and make it to heaven before my friend Joan, I have no doubt those striped shoes will be worn to my funeral. But *if* she should go first, I have worked out a deal with her kids that I will get those shoes, and I will be wearing them to *her* funeral—even if I have to rubber-band them to my feet! She will look down and know I got the last word, and I will look up and smile!

SCANDALOUS SHOeS

Marie Antoinette was known for her love of extravagant, even outlandish, fashion, especially shoes. In fact, she employed a servant whose only duty was to care for her shoes, as well as catalog them by color and style. The ill-fated French queen is said to have owned more than 500 pairs, each custom made for her. After she was convicted of treason in 1793, Marie Antoinette was forbidden to wear a black mourning dress to her death, but she was allowed free reign with regard to footwear. As a result, she rather famously walked to the guillotine wearing a pair of her beloved high heels and stepped on her executioner's foot while wearing them. Her last-known words were: "Monsieur, I beg your pardon; I did not do it on purpose."

Her husband's grandfather, Louis XIV, had been equally fond of high heels in his day— even more so, actually. Though enormous in reputation, power, and presence, the Sun King stood a mere five feet three inches in his bare feet. The diminutive monarch ordered shoes specially made for him with four and five-inch heels from his royal shoemaker Nicholas Lestage. Perhaps to lessen the overtly feminine characteristic of the high-heeled shoes, Lestage depicted intricately drawn battle scenes on the heels of the king's shoes, which were noted not only for their height, but also their color—red.

The shoe-loving Sun King issued a royal edict that wearing shoes with red heels was solely a privilege of the aristocracy, and he also decreed that no one could wear shoes taller than his own. The high tapered heels he frequently wore became so popular (with both men and women) the style is still today referred to as the "Louis Heel." Later, the French Revolution led to the temporary demise of high heels by the well-shod and otherwise. The elevated shoes were seen as symbols of outrageous opulence and were roundly despised by the new hoi polloi who had come into power.

CHAPTER 7

The Basis of All Elegance

There is a reason why the fashion industry has never lost its love for the iconic "little black dress." Classics, as they say, are classics for a reason. Black shoes, black dress, black clutch purse—it's the uniform of sophistication for a woman. The dress gives you an air of feminine mystique and refinement; the clutch (subtly) shows off your rings; and the simple pumps complete the head-to-toe elegance of black on black. They are a shoe-closet staple for women, because they match practically everything, and though they are usually referred to as a wardrobe basic, there is, in fact, nothing basic about a great black shoe. In the South, the perfect black shoe is the equivalent of the little black dress.

Black shoes are always elegant, and because they will never, ever go out of style, a good pair of black heels is one of the wisest wardrobe investments a woman can make. A pair of quality leather black heels will last a lifetime, requiring very little care other than a good buff and polish every now and then. And let me tell you, I can shine a pair of pumps with the best of them. My father made sure of that. Oliver Norton saw to it that none of his children ever left the house without perfectly polished shoes; he said that polished shoes made an outfit and showed that you took pride in how you presented yourself to the world. He was right, too. To this day, shoes are the first things I notice about people, especially women, and if they are wearing black pumps, I feel right off the bat that they are cool, calm, and collected—and that they care about the impression they give others.

Now in my time and place, as a young woman coming of age in the South, black was a color that could not be worn by a woman until she was practically married. After all, it was a major step to wear a black dress with matching pumps. Head-to-toe black meant you had come of age, and that you were ready to don the mantle of womanhood, to dress like more of a mature woman, and that you had something very serious to do and someplace very important to go. I was in college before I ever wore an all-black ensemble; it was the outfit I wore to my first grown-up dinner party. It was in 1973, at a rehearsal dinner for a friend of mine who was getting married. Wearing an 18-inch strand of pearls my mother had chosen for me two years before, a simple but stylish black dress, black stockings, and black heels, I felt so sophisticated, as though I had arrived at a place I had sought to get to for years. I carried myself differently, I talked differently, I felt "put together" in a way I never had before. I felt like I had finally arrived into adulthood, and I had no desire to turn back.

Now that I'm older and more worldly, I know that it isn't necessarily that way in other parts of the country. In New York City, black isn't a wardrobe color. It's the *only* wardrobe color. But growing up in the South, things were different—black was the great fashion divide between girlhood and womanhood. When I was coming of age, young ladies who were fashion-conscious were attired in an array of fresh, bright colors that echoed and changed with the passing seasons. Black was reserved for "adults only," and even that exception is only a few generations old. At one point in time, Southern women would not have dared to wear black unless they were in mourning. In the antebellum South especially, a young belle's pretty, colorful frocks were intended to mirror her sweet nature, and it was simply unheard of for anyone other than ministers or laymen to wear unadorned black in public.

Have you ever seen *Gone with the Wind?* The scene where Scarlett O'Hara shocks Atlanta's finest citizens is one of my favorites in the movie, and it sums up the old-guard Southern attitude about how and when a woman should wear black. In the movie, the scene takes place at a wartime charity ball for the city's military hospital run by Doctor Mead. Scarlett, whose husband has been killed in battle, is attending with all the other young belles of the city. Not in a ball gown, mind you, but in the widow's weeds that etiquette dictates she must wear—no jewelry (other than her wedding ring), no fancy hats, frilly shoes, or pretty frocks, and all black, all over, all the time. For a whole year, or longer! That she has appeared in public while still in mourning is a scandal in and of itself. Her Aunt Pittypat, one of Atlanta's premier social gadflies, is embarrassed to have Scarlett in attendance at all: "For a widow to appear in public at a social gathering, every time I think of it, I feel faint." But Scarlett doesn't care, which is why I love her. The still-in-so-called-mourning Scarlett is just itching to dance—decorum be hanged! And does she ever get her chance.

When a fundraising event allows the gentlemen to bid on dancing partners for twenty-five dollars, blockade runner Rhett Butler stuns them all, boldly offering one-hundred and fifty dollars—in gold—for a twirl with the recently widowed Mrs. Hamilton (take *that* Maybelle Merriweather!). "She will not consider it," the outraged Doctor Mead says. "Oh yes I will," Scarlett shoots back. Aunt Pittypat falls to the floor in a faint when the widow Hamilton races to the dance floor,

> Let your dreams outgrow the shoes of your expectations.
> —Ryunosuke Satoro

her black taffeta skirt billowing around her as she lines up for the Virginia Reel. She doesn't care a fig for the scandal, Scarlett tells Rhett: "I'm going to dance and dance."

To this day in the South, you don't see many little girls or young ladies in either black dresses or black shoes—with one exception. Black patent Mary Janes are the standard-issue shoes for girls ten and under. Very sweet, very feminine, and shiny as a new penny, Mary Janes are not only allowed, but frankly expected for little ones here, and they are paired with smocked dresses mothers make or buy for their daughters. I was no exception, and like my first pair of black pumps later on, my ebony-hued Mary Janes were also shoes that represented the dual nature and power of black shoes. Through shoes especially, the color black epitomizes both childhood and womanhood, innocence and elegance; and a maturity that encompasses sadness, as those in mourning, as well as the joy and adventure of coming into your own as a woman.

Mom bought my first pair of Mary Janes for me; she let me go with her to pick them out. Even at the tender age of six, shoe shopping was a thrill, although not necessarily because of the shoes themselves. These were Red Goose brand shoes, which are no longer made, but which were wildly popular when I was a kid. There was a giant red plastic goose that sat on the counter in the shoe store near the cash register. After your mom or dad paid for your Red Goose shoes, you got to yank that plastic goose's neck down and watch it magically lay a golden egg. Inside was a prize! I remember that mine was a set of jacks that particular time. I was feeling pretty good about my bounty, and I liked the shoes just fine. I was far less certain about the occasion for which they were purchased, however: my first day of school.

Now, first grade for me was a time of trauma. I had come to *like* my routine of being the older sister to my brother and sister and staying home with Mom. We got up, ate cereal while we watched *Captain Kangaroo* and *Romper Room*, then dressed and went out to play. It was the perfect set-up, at least until the day school first loomed before me. Going to school meant Keith and Janice were home having fun, and more important, that I was not. This did not sit well with me. I went, but not without protest. Mom says that I cried everyday for the first two weeks, begging not to go. I don't remember that specifically, but I'm sure it's true. The truth of the matter is I just didn't like school or the changes this new daily regimen brought into my young life.

It wasn't that I didn't like my new friends, but being a student brought about the blinding reality that I was going to have to sit still in a desk all day long, and on top of that, pay attention, mind the teacher, and go by the *rules*. That was intolerable. Structure was the kiss of death for a person like me, and I was much too inquisitive to just take things at face

> Put on your red shoes and let's dance the blues.
> —David Bowie

value. I wanted to know the "whys" behind everything. And if I thought I was missing something, I would do everything I could to get in on it. And if that didn't fit into someone's little rule book, so be it. Or so I led myself to believe.

My first memorable misbehaving experience (notice I said "first") was talking during class. Miss Kelley didn't appreciate having me break her "quiet mouse, still mouse" rules, so she punished me by making me stay inside during recess. That was torture enough. All the other kids got to run around and have fun in the sun while I had to sit still and mute at my desk until they returned. What I didn't realize was that when you broke the rules and stayed inside, a note describing your misdeeds followed you home to your parents. I hadn't really planned on that, and the Norton rule of the house was simple and straightforward: if you are punished at school, you will be punished at home.

> What becomes of the broken-hearted? They buy shoes.
> —Mimi Pond

I was quiet on the ride home. I could actually feel my heart pounding in my chest as Mom drove. The fact that I was so quiet tipped her off immediately that something was not right. As we rode along in our white Buick, I tried to come up with a good story to explain my bad behavior. I thought and thought, but I couldn't come up with anything other than the truth: I liked talking and I always wanted to know what was going on! I handed Mom the note and gave her my side of the story. She accepted my excuses, but told me that I had to settle in at school, and that this change was permanent, so I might as well accept it.

Today, I still struggle with change as so many other women do. Change can be very unsettling to me because I often equate it with losing something precious—familiarity of a routine, the patterns I have created and come to love, and even people. Newness can be exhilarating, yes, but it can also hurt to the core of our being. For this reason, the irony of a pair of black pumps never fails to amaze me.

They are fashion's most steadfast and true accessory. In the world of fashion— where volatile alterations and modifications can and frequently do occur—the status of the black pump is as fixed as the tides. And yet, for me (and for a lot of other women as well, I suspect) little black shoes of one sort or another have always been present for the most profound moments and milestones of change in my life. First day of school shoes, first grown-up lady shoes, and more bittersweet, shoes that also represent the time in my life I lost a friend who I loved deeply.

> The wearer best knows where the shoe pinches.
> —Irish proverb

He was my friend Steve Davis, and he was an incredible man. He was an accomplished, respected physician who truly loved the babies he delivered. He had married one of my closest friends, Melinda, and I decided that if she loved him, then I would too. But when Steve and I got to know each other, it was magic—not to mention the birth of the most aggressive pair of practical jokers on the planet! We would stop at nothing to get at each other. It didn't matter where or when, the object was to play big or go home. It was nothing for Steve to paint Auburn Tiger paw prints on the outside of my Crimson Tide-loving house on Iron Bowl weekends. I, in turn, would call his office the following Monday and pretend to be a banker who just bounced one of his checks! He would get me back by planting posters of me on the outside doors of my office complex, decorated in his own unique style and enhancing my, shall we say, *womanly* attributes. It would take an entire, separate book to tell the stories of our years together and all the terrible, wonderful things we did to each other.

What a friendship! I learned a lot from Steve but the one thing that sank in the most was that you must always express your feelings for the people in your life who you love. Steve called one day with a serious tone in his voice. He wanted to talk, and to tell me that he had been diagnosed with adult non-Hodgkin's lymphoma. I thought he was kidding. He was only thirty-nine years old! But, no, he was serious, and the news just devastated me. Steve sick? No way. But he could fight it, I told myself, there were treatment options.

As the months passed and he began chemotherapy, the treatments began to weaken him, so we would just sit for hours and talk. We even took painting lessons during those times! On his second lesson he decided he was ready to paint portraits and painted the worst and most uncomplimentary rendering of his daughter. She still has not recovered from

High heels are pride and privilege, the passkey to decadence.
—Karen Heller

seeing it. Even when he was gravely ill with cancer, Steve never wanted to stop living, and he never lost the devilish smile that let you know he was up to no good! But the gravity of his illness set in, and he and Melinda made an extended trip to Boston for additional treatments, trying to overcome the cancer in his body. I missed them so much and always looked forward to calling them for an update.

But one evening, Steve called me. He was in the hospital and he told me that Melinda had gone back to her hotel room for the night and he needed to talk. He began by telling me how much he loved me and that our friendship meant the world to him. Tears started streaming down my face and I begged him to stop talking like that, pleading with him not to give up. In his weakened voice, he told me that he knew there would come a time shortly when he would not be able to talk at all. So he called to talk while he still could—about our many years of friendship and our wonderful days spent together planning and pulling pranks on each other. And then he said the most amazing thing, which has stuck with me ever since that night: "I could never let my life end without telling you how much you mean to me". A few days later Melinda called to tell me they were coming home. Steve got home in time to see his loved ones. I went to see him with a rose cut from his own garden. He died the next day, and Melinda asked me if I would play at his funeral.

READER/CUSTOMER CARE SURVEY

HEFG

We care about your opinions! Please take a moment to fill out our online Reader Survey at **http://survey.hcibooks.com.**

As a **"THANK YOU"** you will receive a **VALUABLE INSTANT COUPON** towards future book purchases

as well as a **SPECIAL GIFT** available only online! Or, you may mail this card back to us.

First Name _____ MI. _____ Last Name _____

Address _____ City _____

State _____ Zip _____ Email _____

1. Gender
- ☐ Female   ☐ Male

2. Age
- ☐ 8 or younger
- ☐ 9-12   ☐ 13-16
- ☐ 17-20   ☐ 21-30
- ☐ 31+

3. Did you receive this book as a gift?
- ☐ Yes   ☐ No

4. Annual Household Income
- ☐ under $25,000
- ☐ $25,000 - $34,999
- ☐ $35,000 - $49,999
- ☐ $50,000 - $74,999
- ☐ over $75,000

5. What are the ages of the children living in your house?
- ☐ 0 - 14   ☐ 15+

6. Marital Status
- ☐ Single
- ☐ Married
- ☐ Divorced
- ☐ Widowed

7. How did you find out about the book?
(please choose one)
- ☐ Recommendation
- ☐ Store Display
- ☐ Online
- ☐ Catalog/Mailing
- ☐ Interview/Review

8. Where do you usually buy books?
(please choose one)
- ☐ Bookstore
- ☐ Online
- ☐ Book Club/Mail Order
- ☐ Price Club (Sam's Club, Costco's, etc.)
- ☐ Retail Store (Target, Wal-Mart, etc.)

9. What subject do you enjoy reading about the most?
(please choose one)
- ☐ Parenting/Family
- ☐ Relationships
- ☐ Recovery/Addictions
- ☐ Health/Nutrition
- ☐ Christianity
- ☐ Spirituality/Inspiration
- ☐ Business Self-help
- ☐ Women's Issues
- ☐ Sports

10. What attracts you most to a book?
(please choose one)
- ☐ Title
- ☐ Cover Design
- ☐ Author
- ☐ Content

BUSINESS REPLY MAIL
FIRST-CLASS MAIL PERMIT NO 45 DEERFIELD BEACH, FL

POSTAGE WILL BE PAID BY ADDRESSEE

Health Communications, Inc.
3201 SW 15th Street
Deerfield Beach FL 33442-9875

FOLD HERE

Comments

I remember the sound of my black heels clicking down the center aisle of the church as I made my way to the piano to play Steve's favorite hymns before the service. The traditional garb of mourning—basic black pumps with a simple black suit—was, for me, also the dress of celebration. While my heart was breaking, I also clung to our last conversation. In that one phone call, I had learned one of life's most beautiful lessons from Steve: I learned the power of words. Expression of gratitude and love is essential to those in your life. If you are too timid to speak your feelings, write them, but get them out there! Before that conversation, too many times I had let distractions or time commitments or work or whatever get in the way of stopping to express my thoughts and feelings to those I care about and love. Steve's words changed that; they changed my life. I still miss him today, but I cherish his carefully placed words.

And I'm learning to embrace the dual—not to mention inevitable—nature of change. How can I avoid it? I look in the mirror and things are really changing! The young girl with untested dreams and unsure expectations who once looked back at me is gone and in her place is a woman who has lived enough years to see some of those hopeful longings realized and some of them dashed against the rocks. But like the always relevant, ever-present pair of black pumps, I'm still *here*—a little broken in, perhaps, but in top form! In fact, I'm better than ever. And that's what counts.

> High heels were invented by a woman who had been kissed on the forehead.
> —Christopher Morley

MEMENTO MORI

The late Queen Victoria of England was one of the most influential women in history, the face and impetus behind one of the most creative, inspired eras of our time—the Victorian Age. Her Royal Majesty set the standard for many social dictates and customs that still reign today, including wearing black as a public symbol and statement of mourning. After her beloved consort, Prince Albert, died of typhoid fever in 1861, the queen went into seclusion, wearing only black dresses (some lightened by a touch of white lace) for the remainder of her life. Queen Victoria's abject grief and limited public appearances earned her a new nickname, the Widow of Windsor.

The dutiful Victorians followed their queen's example, emulating her *"memento mori."* Widows, who were expected to remain in mourning for at least a period of two years, wore only black in public—right down to their parasols, hair accessories, fans, and shoes. Even their kerchiefs and personal stationery were etched in black! Silk crepe, a somewhat flat, lusterless fabric, was the most popular choice for garments of the bereaved, who were also expected to wear a jet-black "weeping veil" for a year, and to limit public outings to mostly church services. "Full mourning" lasted a year, followed by a slightly less rigorous "second mourning," which afforded the addition of basic embellishments back into the wardrobe, such as trims and simple jewelry. In the final six months, the period known by Victorians as "half-mourning," colors could fashionably expand to include simple, somber hues, such as grey, and all manner of jewelry was deemed acceptable.

Rite of Passage

There are many moments in a young woman's life that mark a Rite of Passage, that help bridge the gap between girlishness and womanhood. For many of us, it was having our ears pierced (an event that in the Norton household was preceded by a sixteenth birthday and copious amounts of begging); for others it was purchasing that first tube of red lipstick; and for a few, that moment is achieved with a new, chic, all-grown-up new hairstyle, complete with highlights that have been chemically enhanced just enough to look natural. For me, it was zipping into my first pair of white go-go boots.

For those of you who are unfortunate enough to have missed it, *That Girl* was a hugely popular comedy that ran on ABC from 1966 to 1971. Starring Marlo Thomas as the happily single, frankly fashionable Ann Marie, that show did for go-go boots what Jackie Kennedy had done for pill-box hats just a few years earlier. I, along with every other teen-aged girl in America, was glued to the tube every week watching that show and drooling over Ann Marie's Fifth-Avenue wardrobe and glamorous career as an actress trying to break into the business. The opening credits would roll, and suddenly there was Marlo Thomas running through Central Park flying a kite, wearing a phenomenal minidress, made up to Mod perfection, her perfect flip hairstyle blowing just right in the breeze. Hollywood, don't you love it!

For girls my age, though, *That Girl* was the emblem of our collective future. She was single, beautiful, living alone while dating the scrumptious Donald Hollinger, and pursuing that ever-elusive acting career. I wouldn't have missed that show for anything. Fashion was dictated by this woman. Why, the episode where Ann Marie got her first pair of dangly, chandelier earrings absolutely set the tone for all women of the day. Lou Marie, her dad, presented them to her when he felt she was "ready." It was her Rite of Passage. But the real fashion icon to emerge from the show, especially for me, were the snow-white, calf-hugging go-go boots that made Marlo's wardrobe full of minidresses just *pop*.

Once my sister Janice and I got a look at those way-too-trendy boots, we fell in love with them. White patent leather, zipped up the side and a small stacked heel—the picture of cool. Janice and I would visit them at department stores as if they were long-lost friends and dream of how we would look exactly like the effervescent Ann Marie if we ever got a pair. We had one small obstacle to overcome, though. Come to think if it, maybe not so small. That was the "Big O", one Oliver Norton, our dad. Now, Dad is a man who spoiled his girls, but when it came to real trendy things, he took a wait-and-see atti- tude. In his estimation, putting our family money toward things that lasted was more important and yielded more permanent results. I agreed with him too . . . except when it came to those go-go boots, when all reason and logic went right out the window.

> Nothing has been invented yet that will do a better job than high heels at making a good pair of legs look great, or great ones look fabulous.
> —Stuart Weitzman

We campaigned tirelessly, Janice and I. We hinted that these boots would be the perfect addition to our wardrobes and would match everything we had in our closets, making them terribly *economical*. We even tried to convince Mom to overlook the inviolate "no white shoes after Labor Day" rule. No dice. Next, we pulled out the big guns. We tried the tried-and-true Norton sibling method fondly known as the "Janice in his lap" approach. She is the baby and when Keith or I really wanted to get an answer from the "Big O," and we really, really wanted that answer to be yes, we put the baby up to selling the idea. That didn't work either. As a last-ditch effort, we even put on the old "everyone but us has them" line, only to find the non-breachable response of: "If everyone jumped off a cliff, would you do it too?" My answer was quick and sure: "Well frankly, for these boots I might consider it!" Babysitting for extra spending money to pay for them ourselves was also an option we considered. But after putting my future CPA's brain to the test, I determined that for the one dollar we each made per hour, Janice and I would have to quit school and babysit full time for every family in the neighborhood to pay for those boots!

Little did we know that Mom had purchased them for our Christmas gift that year and had them hidden away (she had two go-to hidey-holes—the top of her closet and the trunk of her car). I don't know how she kept a straight face with our boot campaign in full swing on a daily basis. Nevertheless, on Christmas morning, there they were! We opened them at the same time and immediately put them on with our Christmas pajamas. I felt like the Queen of Cool! I pranced around in those boots all day long, planning my wardrobe, soon to be filled with jazzy little hats, oversized accessories, and A-line skirts that would make those boots—and me—look like the carefree but single-minded sophisticate I knew I could now become.

> Sometimes you have to sacrifice your performance for high heels.
> —Gwen Stefani

Life was complete and when we returned to school, Janice and I marched around like little ducks in our white go-go boots, along with everyone else who had gotten them for Christmas. Our Rite of Passage had occurred. We had passed from childhood into almost-adulthood in those white go-go boots and Mom and Dad had been transformed from ordinary to cool parents. I was in control of my destiny at last. Ha! Little did I know about the lesson that another, very different pair of boots would teach me later in life about the meaning of the word "control."

I was to learn this lesson in Montana at the ripe age of 53. Montana is one of the most beautiful states I have ever seen: breathtaking vistas, rolling hills, and blue cloudless skies. My friends, Suzanne and Michael Blum, went to Nine Quarter Circle Ranch, a dude ranch in Gallatin Gateway, Montana, every summer and took their girls for a week of riding, roping, and enjoying the great outdoors. The girls, Catherine, Caroline, and Alexandra, are adorable, excellent riders, and looked fabulous in their skinny blue jeans. Needing a break, my husband, Wayne, and I accepted our friends' invitation to go with them, and I remember how much we were, at the time, looking forward to experiencing a different type of vacation from any other we had enjoyed in the past. I immediately started thinking about the types of clothes and shoes I would need, when it occurred to me I would *have* to have boots. Riding boots! I knew that the itinerary at the ranch would include a daily morning ride, and I was certainly not going to be outdone by the old hands or show up looking like a greenhorn.

I located the perfect pair of boots online after searching and searching and wading through endless websites that promised vast selections of "equestrian-class" boots with features that sounded important, like "cushioned insoles, side zips, and soft knit linings." The pair I finally settled on were beauts—black leather, calf-length boots with slick soles, which, I learned, were more of a vital safety measure than a fashionable accent. The thick, treadless soles made it easy for the rider's feet to slip out of the stirrups in the event of being thrown off the horse. That gave me a little pause, but I figured if you looked the part, you could do anything.

When the gigantic box came, I tore into it and tried them on. In my mind, I traveled back in time to yet another television show starring a well-shod, boots-loving heroine: this time *Big Valley*, a western that starred a very young, very blond, pre-Dynasty-era Linda Evans, who, in every show, came riding up on her perfectly behaved horse with hair and makeup intact. That would be me in Montana.

Not diamonds, but heels are a girl's best friends.
—William Rossi

We got there and checked into our rustic little cabin, emphasis on the "rustic." I looked around the ranch and quickly realized that there was no room service, no spa, and no television. For one full week, I was going to be a rancher.

No, seriously. The first evening we were there, the dinner bell rang and we all assembled in the dining hall to get our grub and receive our instructions for the next day's itinerary, beginning with the morning ride . . . When the ranch hands asked us individually to select what experience level we were at as riders, I suddenly realized that we were the only adult newcomers to ranch-life in the room. *Uhhhhmmmm*, this was not looking so good. I'm fairly certain I heard a snicker or two when the lady's magazine-publishing, lipstick-wearing gal from Alabama was faced with the fairly foreign task of riding a horse, but little did *they* know, *I* had it all together. I had a plan, albeit, an unorthodox one: I could just ride with the children! I had packed my boots and my brand-spanking-new, ten-gallon, black cowboy hat, thank you very *much*. It even sported a rhinestone tiara that sat right on front above the brim. My silver-studded black suede riding jacket with fringes and crisp new blue jeans would complete my ensemble for the next morning's ride. I wanted to ride with the children's group, a request that was unequivocally, and I thought unfairly, denied, so I selected the "novice" level ride.

I'm not waiting forever to get those shoes!
—*Wicked Witch of the West*

At work and in my personal life, I was used to calling the shots, so being a novice was new to me. The positions we occupy from 9 to 5 dictate the impressions we give other people. On a ranch if you *look* like a cowgirl, assumptions might be made that you *are* one, but the proof, as in all things, lies in the pudding, as they say. I quickly realized what I had gotten myself into, and that perhaps I had bitten off more than I could chew, but the inner being in me demanded that I shake off the fear of entering this new, wildly unfamiliar territory. I decided I was going to get on that horse if it killed me. Turns out, it almost did.

After a very, very short night's sleep of sleeping with one eye open and two ears cocked for the sound of the wild animals I felt sure were going to break in and maul me any minute, the breakfast bell finally rang at the crack of dawn. It seemed as though we had entered a new time zone, "mountain time," so dawn seemed especially early that day, despite the fact that I'm naturally an early riser. I moseyed up to the front porch of the dining hall and sat there in the frigid morning air drinking coffee and contemplating my first ride. As the horses were being brought around it occurred to me that I had not been on a horse since I was a child and not only were they big, they did not come with brakes. After a full cowgirl's breakfast of eggs, bacon, and biscuits, I was feeling slightly nauseated when they brought my horse, Benjamin, around. The old boy was saddled up and ready to go. As the ranch hands demonstrated how to mount the gigantic beasts by *flinging* one's body up and into the saddle—all in one smooth motion—I realized that both my flinging ability and my horse-riding skills could use some work. To make matters worse, everyone had to saddle up in the front of the barn where all could see. Could there be anything worse than saddling up in public, I wondered, before settling on the idea that, no, there was not in fact anything worse. What are barns for anyway? Couldn't we *fling* just easily *behind* the barn?

My turn finally came and I proceeded to saddle up. I asked for a step-ladder, but they wouldn't give me one, explaining step-by-step how to properly saddle up: Foot in stirrup, hands on the saddle horn, then you jump, pull up, and swing

your body onto the back of the horse and into the saddle—
all in one fluid motion. It looked so easy and graceful when
Linda Evans did it on *Big Valley*. I can tell you from experience that, in real life, hopping on a horse is a true athlete's
feat. As I tried to get all my parts moving at once, the horse
and I were getting off on an equally bad foot.

> Between
> saying and doing,
> many a pair of shoes
> is worn out.
> —Iris Murdoch

The relationship between me and old
Benjamin was anything but love at first
sight; his idea of love language and my
idea of love language (quickly growing to include the phrase "blasted
horse") didn't match up. As I struggled
to get a firm grip on both saddle and stirrup, he just stood there and looked at me like "get
it over with." I was starting to really hate that horse, but I
finally managed to get up on him. Michael has a wonderful
photo of me (taken from behind) as I flung my body almost
gracefully into the saddle. I have, over the years, considered
offering him a great deal of money to destroy that picture
and the negatives too, to no avail.

Things still weren't going too smoothly with Benjamin
either. That horse did everything he could to make me look
bad. He wouldn't listen, he bull-headedly refused to go forward, and he stopped to eat continually, munching on the
grass, an act that was followed by the inevitable, well . . .
you know.

At the ranch hand's instruction, I kicked Benjamin to get

him going. I figured he would get mad and buck me off, but no, he managed to stop eating and you-knowing for five seconds and get moving. We started out of the pen on a very narrow path. I had a death grip on the reins; my hands ached from holding on so tight, sweating from nervousness inside my leather riding gloves. I was so attuned to the unfamiliar, jarring movements of the gargantuan animal beneath me that I did not notice that we were going up a razor-steep mountain until I looked down. Had I mistakenly gotten on the wrong tour? This had to be an advanced trek for daredevils who *wanted* to die young. I didn't want to die at all. Pinkie swear. We kept going up, and up, and up. It seemed to take forever as we were headed toward the top. All the while I was hanging on the side of a mountain, sitting on a horse who didn't like me (the feeling was mutual!), and peering down into a deep ravine knowing I would never survive the fall if I fell off the back of old Benjamin. When I finally got to the crest, I was amazed to find myself still in one piece, and I took a minute to just look around at the magnificent countryside in the valleys below and take in the glorious, God-created wonder of it all. There I was, in my first pair of riding boots, transformed into the Queen of Cool. I had conquered my fear, tamed the wild beast of horse that had brought me here, and I was perfectly at peace now that the paralyzing ride up the mountain was over. I was (and it sort of felt like literally) on top of the world!

Then it happened, that defining moment of truth—the

one where I found out for sure that, like the old Blood, Sweat,
and Tears song said, what goes up must come down. I was on
top of one of the highest mountains I had ever seen, on the
back of a stubborn horse named Benjamin
who didn't seem overly fond of me, and .
. . we were off. As we started down, old
Benjamin broke into a gallop. A *fast*
gallop, which to me felt like warp
speed. Now, interestingly enough, my
fellow riders later told me that, in reality, Benjamin was trotting more than gal-
loping, but to me it felt like warp speed. Either
way, the horse was now in charge and it was he who was
setting the pace, leaving me little choice but to sit pitched
forward in the saddle, hanging on for all I was worth, eyes
bulging out of my head, the wind whistling in my ears like a
siren as we went downward. My rational brain ceased to
function and a sense of panic set in.

If you rebel against
high heels take care
to do so in a
very smart hat.
—George Bernard Shaw

I screamed "whoa" as loud as I could several times while
hanging on for dear life, silently confessing my sins and praying for mercy. One of the ranch hands rode up beside me,
and I suddenly got a feeling that he had done this before,
and, somehow, through the thick fog of fear that seemed to
envelop me, the words he was yelling at me sank in: "He
thinks you are saying GO." I immediately quit yelling
"whoa." As woman and horse descended, my life continued
to pass before my eyes, but I could also see the steep cliffs

passing rapidly behind me as that cranky old horse proceeded toward home base. Back at the barn, he finally
stopped. I thought I would cry, though whether from sheer
relief or lingering terror I still cannot say.

I am happy to report that my shiny boots looked fabulous,
my cowboy hat rested steadily, albeit, crookedly, on top of
my head, my signature red lipstick, only slightly chewed off,
was still in place, and my dignity while not as put together
as my Eddie Bauer catalogue ensemble, remained intact
enough for me to deem the whole thing a success.

I still sort of hated that horse, but I figured since I was
going to have to saddle up again the next day with old
Benjamin, I might as well at least tolerate him for the time
being. He had, after all, only *tried* to kill me. He hadn't suc-
ceeded, so I decided in my largesse to forgive and forget,
maybe even save him a sugar cube or two from the dining
hall, and drive the words "glue factory" right out of my con-
scious thoughts. All in all, it was "mission accomplished." I
had made it!

Just like when I was coming down that mountain on top of
a horse I had never met before, there have been many times
in my life that it seemed things were perfectly in place and
other times when everything from the ground up has seemed
completely out of control. That no matter where I was,
things were coming down around me at such a rapid pace
that I couldn't get control of my emotions. In times of stress
and turmoil, we tend to search for answers in the drama of it

all, and there are times when those answers don't immediately present themselves. Sometimes, you just have to hang on to the horse and wait for the wild ride to end, even if you develop carpal tunnel from all the clenching.

How many times do the pressures of work and family send us seeking quick fixes to make problems disappear? We women love for things to get "fixed" fast so our lives will quickly fall back into our comfortable groove, which is just as often a rut, though we can't see that at the time. The truth is, we just never know what is around the bend or how our lives can be disrupted so quickly. What's more, what feels like disruption may actually turn out to be a welcome change.

When that happens, take time to retreat and reclaim your thoughts. Allow yourself to simply sit and breathe. Whatever you are dealing with today, it will pass from you. The good news is you will be stronger for it in the end. And remember, even when you're on the back of a bucking bronco of a horse, dig in your heels and hang on! With a little determination and a lot of faith, you'll make it through in one piece. Take it from me, ladies, sometimes you have to just ride it out. And when you can, take that ride in spiffy new boots and a tiara. It will make all the difference.

ALL BOOTS ARe NOT CReATeD eQUAL

There is a world of difference between American "cowboy" boots and classic English leather riding boots. Less stylized than cowboy boots, the English-style boot features a tall, knee-length shaft, a sturdy rounded, reinforced toe, and a low to moderate heel. The high-reaching shaft protects the rider's leg from being pinched by the leather saddle, while the heel prevents the foot from slipping forward into the stirrup. English-style "dress boots" (worn by dressage riders, show jumpers, and fox hunters) are typically black and have a stiffer ankle than field boots, which often feature lacing at the ankle for more flexibility.

Unlike their smooth-leather, English cousins, western-style boots are typically calf-length with a slightly higher angled heel and pointed toe (except "roper" boots, which have a rounded toe). Cowboy boots are most often made of leather, but are also available in other exotic materials, which range from ostrich hide to rattlesnake skins. The popular boots are frequently embellished with decorative Western-style stitching and sometimes accessorized with spurs attached to the heel and used by the rider to cue the horse.

CHAPTER 9

Staying in Step

I have always said that, in this world, there are casual acquaintances and there are keepers—the kind of friends you can be completely transparent with and with whom you can share your innermost thoughts and feelings, knowing in your heart that you are safe in loving hands. By the same comparison, and on a lighter note, there are fashion followers and there are fashion setters. And almost immediately upon bursting on the world scene in the early eighties, Lady Diana Spencer secured her place in the latter category. Diana was one of the most refreshing faces to have come along in decades (regardless of her final years or the scandal that surrounded the royal family). At first, the shy young Sloane Ranger appeared in the popular apparel of her peers:

modest, high-necked blouses and
skirts, country manor tweeds, ruffled
dresses, and barely-there low heels.
When she became Diana, Princess of
Wales, however, she took to her new
role as a fashion plate and trendsetter like
a model to the runway. And like every
other woman on the planet between
the ages of twenty and eighty, my
best friend Barbara and I couldn't
get enough.

   We drooled over the young British
royal, who almost single-handedly
ignite the designer handbag industry and who helped revive
the art of millinery. Though my mother had always worn
hats—pillboxes and veiled toppers were her favorites—
young ladies of my generation had long since discarded cha-
peaux in favor of more modern accessories. Lady Di changed
all that. Together, Barbara and I pored over magazines and
books with her pictures splashed in them and marveled at
her always perfectly coordinated wardrobe, from the shoes
on her feet to the matching hat on her head, and the smashing colored hose that always tied her whole look together.
We felt a real kinship with the young royal, who favored
romantically ruffled collars, pearl chokers, silks, satins, and
darling little suits. We even both got her famous haircut, the
layered pageboy that was so popular it became known simply

as the "Lady Di." Diana was one of the first fashionistas to master the art of wearing monochromatic color schemes—red was an oft-worn favorite—and she was the first woman in this century, besides nurses in uniform, to wear white stockings. We adored the way she wore pearls and hats, and even though she was probably too young for the styles she tried to pull off, we admired her chic spirit. She was trying to fit in while still make her mark on her new world! She definitely looked the part of a princess, but she did it with a youthful vigor and style that set the whole world on its ear.

Of course, it was all about the shoes for me. They drew me to her. Diana tended to favor little kitten heels, but she upped the oomph factor by choosing shoes in a rainbow of hues the likes of which the fashion world had not previously seen. In a world of navy and black stilettos and plain old pumps, Diana stood out from the crowd wearing shoes in fresh, exciting colors in every shade and tone: blues, pinks, yellows, greens . . . you name it. They looked fabulous with her matching hats and handbags. What a collection! By the early nineties—and this is a documented fact—the dashing Di had amassed more than 200 purses and 250 pairs of shoes. Can you imagine? I can only dream about her dressing room.

During the Lady Diana era (which began in 1981 and exists even today, as her influence is still felt in the fashion world), whenever we got the chance to visit each other, Barbara and I made special trips to local malls here in Birmingham and near Barbara's home in Gastonia, North Carolina, to find wonderful shoes just like those the princess wore. And one day just before Easter, one of our jaunts proved a smashing success. Right in the middle of the usual spring whites, creams, and black patent leather T-straps were these incredible peach pumps, complete with the requisite Lady Di one-and-a-half-inch heel. And to make it even better, the store had a pair in each of our sizes. Since Barbara lived in North Carolina and I in Birmingham, we figured it didn't matter that our shoes matched! If anything, it delighted us.

We found hats in matching colors that day as well, an absolute fashion necessity in the South. Hats may have gone in and out of style over the years, but a Southern lady wouldn't dare be caught on Easter Sunday without a proper bonnet. We start wearing them young too; there's a picture of me in the family at age three taken in Montgomery on Easter Sunday. There is a tiny hat on my head, and a little strap under my chin, holding it in place and covering my curls, which were courtesy of a Toni Home Permanent. Ask any Southern woman between the ages of 40 and 60 whether her mother ever tortured her with a Toni perm when she was little, and odds are the answer will be "yes."

> I've always looked at shoes as being immensely beautiful things.
> *Graham Coxon*

For this particular Easter, my friend Barbara had lucked into a cute tri-corner hat with a fabulous ostrich feather that reached from the brim to the back. She had the Diana look down pat. My own hat was not in a style Diana had worn, but it was equally stunning! It was a portrait-style hat with a silk bow in the back and a large brim that spanned the width of the shoulders. It's a style I still favor today (perfect for having your picture taken because it frames your face) and one that always makes me feel glamorous and regal when I wear it.

That Easter Sunday, Barbara and I called each other after services and compared notes on our dual Lady Di looks at our respective churches. Apparently we both had made excellent choices, as we had each received countless compliments from fellow members of our congregations. I noted with interest that many of the kind words came from gentleman, who commented how happy they were to see the return of women wearing hats in church and in general—and not just at Easter. Though the "shampoo and set" trend of our mothers' generation may have passed, they said, (this was when Southern women had their hair "fixed" once a week at the local beauty shop), the resurgence of such a feminine trend was refreshing, they told me. Aglow from all the compliments and good cheer, that Easter Sunday passed pleasantly enough for me in Birmingham and for Barbara in Gastonia, and after I got home from church and changed into more casual clothes for the day, I carefully packed my Lady Di shoes away in protective reams of tissue for future wear.

I didn't think about either again until one evening a few months later, when my phone rang. Barbara was on the other end of the line, and the news she called to share with me was devastating. Her house in Gastonia had burned that day, and she and her family had essentially lost everything but their lives. I had to sit down and collect my thoughts. Everyone was fine, she assured me, but to experience something like this was overwhelming for her, especially with a daughter and son in junior high, a second daughter who was still in grade school, and a husband in tow. She and her family were in a hotel, she said, and they would be unable to even return to the house until the following day to look for any of their belongings that might be salvageable.

A couple of weeks later, after Barbara and her family had settled into a temporary rental manse made available through the church Jim pastored, I went to visit to help her get the children ready for the start of a new school year. In a spare room in the rental house, there were several things that had been pulled from the ruins of her former home, among them the tri-corner hat and peach pumps. They had been all but melted by the fire but were still recognizable. It gave us a good laugh to recall our incredible luck of finding matching peach-colored shoes.

After the kids were in bed that night, and her husband Jim had retreated to his study, Barbara and I had coffee and talked about the fire, and how she had to start over from scratch with everything, from the basic necessities to those luxuries she had come to love, like the needlework that she had spent a lifetime creating. A gifted artist, Barbara had spent years stitching intricate, one-of-a-kind samplers, all of which had been destroyed. Her beautiful handwork had turned to dust before her eyes when she sifted through the wreckage the day after the fire, found them, and touched them, hoping against hope that even one might have survived the flames. Also gone were Jim's exquisite collection of watercolor paintings of birds and wildlife, a hobby and collection he would now have to begin anew.

Through tears, Barbara told me about picking up her youngest daughter Emily from school the day of the fire and rounding the corner of her street only to see her two oldest and clearly terrified children standing there with fully-suited firemen. Barbara had cried with relief, she said, when she realized that everyone in her family was unharmed, and she wept again when she recounted those terrifying, life-changing moments. I cried with her when she talked about the genuine and understandable grief she felt at losing those things that could never be replaced, including personal keepsakes such as album upon album of baby and wedding pictures. She was my "keeper," and I hers, and I tried to comfort my dear friend whose voice trembled as she bared her truest and most uninhibited feelings and emotions to me, and I tried to make her laugh too, because laughter through tears is often the best kind.

The peach shoes came up again, as did beaucoups of oohing and aahing over Lady Diana's latest fashionable escapades. This was in 1983, and Diana had *just* made headlines wearing peach, this time in Canada in a period gown nicknamed the "Klondike Dress" by the press. The princess-line silk gown with a swag overskirt and matching hat (naturally!) had been made especially for Diana by Oscar-winning costume designer John Bright. The young princess had worn the nineteenth century-style attire just two days before her twenty-second birthday at a costumed barbecue for the historic re-creation of Fort Edmonton.

As we dished about Diana's Canadian outing like two young star-struck girls, Barbara pulled a blueberry trifle she had prepared for dessert out of the fridge. There's not a Southern woman worth her sugar bowl who doesn't own at least one good trifle dish, a deep pedestal bowl intended not only to hold but also to showcase the colorful layers of cake or ladyfingers, thick custard, and fresh fruit. This one, by necessity, was served in a plastic Tupperware bowl, and it remains to this day the most heavenly blueberry trifle I have ever put in my mouth. I can still close my eyes and taste every delicious bite of the creamy vanilla custard, the sherry-soaked ladyfingers, and the plump, tart blueberries that burst on my tongue with every bite.

As we talked, kicked our feet up, and feasted on blueberry

> I like to literally put women on a pedestal.
> —Vivienne Westwood

trifle served on borrowed dishes out of a plastic bowl, we realized that it wasn't the loss of Barbara's precious peach shoes that was worth remembering or even that fabulous little tri-corner hat, but rather the fun we had experienced shopping together as friends. Friendship was what made those peach pumps so special—the sisterhood of shoes. As an act of solidarity, I came home to Birmingham and vowed never to wear mine again, and I haven't. The survivor's guilt would be too much for me, knowing hers were gone! Barbara is my oldest and dearest friend, you see, and she has stayed in step with me through the great milestones of my life for as long as I can remember

When I first met Barbara, she and her husband were living next door to my then-fiancé, Wayne, in Cullman, Alabama. I was up from Birmingham, visiting, and preparing for my move there. Having been told by Wayne when I would be visiting, she knocked on the door, introduced herself to me, and invited me over for afternoon coffee. I was absolutely charmed, and an instant kinship and mutual respect began right then and there. And has she ever turned out to be a "keeper," in every way I can think of. With Barbara, I can relax and be myself, whether it's joy or heartbreak time. I can tell her how I really feel about anyone or anything, and she has stayed in step with me for more than thirty years now. I can't imagine my life without her. "God made you especially for me," I tell her, and I mean it.

It was Barbara who helped set the course for my career.

She, along with my sister Janice, helped me found Symbol of Excellence Publishers, with Barbara overseeing the editorial, Janice handling circulation, and me managing the rest. It began with a conversation at my kitchen table. As passionate needle workers, Barbara and I realized there was no magazine on the market that catered to our hobby. So we started one—*Just CrossStitch*. It was a risk, but a calculated one, and they took that leap of faith with me. I knew that if we could get 3,000 subscribers inside of a year, we could make it. If not, we could return the money to subscribers, no harm, no foul. We were overwhelmed when the subscription cards started pouring in! By the second issue, we had 25,000 subscribers and the beginnings of a career that would see us publish other magazines and books together, sell the company, buy it back, and start all over with me running Hoffman Media and Barbara taking the helm of several of the company's most successful start-ups. She is still today one of Hoffman's most seasoned editors, overseeing both the birth of a quickly growing niche title, *TeaTime*, and the rebirth of the almost cult-status *Victoria*.

> High heels are pride and privilege, the passkey to decadence.
> —*Karen Heller*

But it hasn't been all work and no play with me and Barb. With her blond hair, delicate china-doll complexion, and beautiful blues eyes, Barbara is the very picture of elegance and graciousness— the kind of woman who apologizes when serving you trifle out of Tupperware, no matter *what* the circumstances. And though you'd never know it to look at her, Barbara is a not only a fanatic about sweets in general, she is inordinately fond of one of my own personal favorites, Krispy Kreme doughnuts! Now, fried flour and sugar is tough to beat in any form, but throw some yeast in the mix and you've got a sure-fire winner, which is why Krispy Kreme has cornered the market on doughnuts south of the Mason-Dixon.

About a decade ago, not too long after we had gotten the magazine *Southern Lady* off the ground, I flew to North Carolina one afternoon for a visit. Barbara was working as an editor for two of our needlework titles at the time, and between keeping the momentum going on her end and mine, we hadn't had a lot of time to just sit and catch up. But as soon as I got in Barbara's car at the airport, it was just like old times, and she couldn't wait to tell me in a conspiratorial tone that a new Krispy Kreme doughnut shop had just opened in her neighborhood. Her favorite time of day was when the red neon "Hot Now" sign was glowing. For those of you unfamiliar with the Krispy Kreme schedule, that sign is turned on when a fresh batch of doughnuts is rolling off the line in the back where they make them. They come to you still warm from the fryer, drenched in a dense, sugary glaze that you have to taste to believe.

The grand opening was in progress when we pulled up, and the promotional feature was a BOGO, buy one, get one free (an ad slogan now tied to Payless Shoes and one that I can associate with two of my favorite things in life). So as we made our way to the drive-thru, Barbara suggested that we take them up on their offer and grab a dozen of the warm delicacies so we would receive a complimentary free dozen. In customary contradictory fashion, she ordered two Diet Cokes just in case we might want to eat a doughnut on the way home. When the cashier handed us the boxes of piping hot donuts, we decided it would be only fitting to enjoy a couple while they were at their peak of freshness. The fact that we had both missed lunch made it an easy decision, giving us just the excuse we needed to enjoy every bite.

As the thirty-minute ride to her home continued, we were talking and laughing and absolutely inhaling the Krispy Kremes one by one, washing them down with Diet Coke. When we pulled into her driveway, we looked down at the box and broke into tearful laughter. It was empty, save for a few sugary crumbs! One dozen gone in a flash, much to our giddy embarrassment.

We decided to keep this little piece of information to our over-indulgent selves and to simply take in the BOGO box of doughnuts that had somehow managed to escape our grasp. We got out of the car and brushed the glazed crumbs off our shelves (that is chests, for those of you outside of the South), discarded the empty box in the trash can, and wobbled into the house. Her husband Jim was already home, and we exchanged greetings. Barbara set the box down and told Jim we would have doughnuts for dessert after supper. Jim insisted that we sit down have a cup of coffee and a doughnut, then a late supper. Barbara and I pushed our doughnuts around on our plates, trying not to let the nausea we felt at the thought of eating another doughnut show on our faces. It took several long minutes and many tiny bites to eat that treat! And it took months before either one of us wanted a doughnut again.

But that's what dear friends do. They stick with you— through the laughter and the tears, the peach shoes, and the doughnuts—and they help you make it along the journey. When you have a friendship like that, you must nurture it. I think there are very few people in your lifetime who you can take into your total confidence, with whom everything just "clicks." Such relationships are based on the meeting of souls, and these are the keepers who become part of what I call the "inner circle," those few special companions to whom you can reveal *anything*, who will help you polish off the BOGO box of doughnuts before giving up your secrets and who stay with you every step of the way, no matter where the road leads!

And just as I flew to her side so long ago when catastrophe struck, my friend has done the same for me, very recently actually. Barbara was there for one of the greatest milestones of my life, the beginning of my marriage, and she has been here for me through the end of it as well. In fact, fittingly enough, it was Barbara who chose my "Starting Over" shoes. In my signature colors of black, red, and white, they are precious little black-and-white printed pumps with red trim and a red double grosgrain bow. We were both attracted to those shoes when we spotted them at a shoe store during a business trip to Williamsburg, Virginia. They are so sassy and have such attitude, and just the right pair to help me start out on this new road.

Today I find myself in a much different place than where I thought I would be when I started my journey into adulthood. Thirty years ago when I left home to marry, I never once thought about a divorce in my future. This is a path that I never even thought about walking. So many women find themselves in this situation by choice or by no-choice. Either way, it is indeed a path where you really find out who you are, and who can go the last mile with you. As women, we give so much away—to our children, our spouses, our co-workers, or anyone else who calls on us—that sometimes at the end of the day there is nothing of ourselves left to give, and we find that our inner strength is zapped and the well is nearly dry. Most of us see ourselves as the "fix-it" people. We spend a large portion of our days helping others untangle their own knots, so much so that sometimes we lose sight of our own wants and needs. And that's not necessarily a bad thing. Many times, in helping others work through their own situations, we gain the necessary experience and

> Shoes, like buildings, have a mysterious chemistry of proportion.
> —Suzanne Slesin

confidence to help us find our own solutions when life's myriad problems come knocking at our doors. And while I hope that I will please the people in my life and make their day better when our paths cross, the bottom line is this: I can only control me. What other people think or do is a result of their choices. The biggest things I have learned are that you can't make someone love you, in any kind of relationship, be it romantic or otherwise, and you don't always have to have the answers. Sometimes just being there and walking beside those you love is enough.

> A buckle is a great addition to an old shoe.
> —*Irish proverb*

Time and age have taught me the enormous power of new beginnings. Today, I am, by description, a "divorcee," it's true. But I am also the CEO of a major publishing company, a mother, and the grandmother of an enchanting baby boy, whose gleaming eyes can melt butter. He is my family's perfect new beginning. I always dreamed I would be a grandmother one day, but until it happens you can't describe it. You see a little bit of your life pass by when you watch your own child become a parent, and you wonder to yourself how in the world they are going to raise this child when they are still children themselves. Then one day I watched my son, Eric, and my lovely daughter-in-law, Katie, with little Hays. I realized they are phenomenal parents and that this little boy will have everything he needs to grow into a wonderful man like his dad.

"New beginnings" is a phrase that I have heard for years.
But I have never really known what it means until now. I
wake up and try to find a familiar path, knowing that today
there will be new paths, an idea which does not frighten me.
I know that new paths bring new adventures, sometimes
challenges, but always different scenery to take in. I was married for 30 years, and when I took those vows, I never
thought it would end this way.

I know people who have let divorce or other life disasters,
such as the death of a loved one or a fire that robbed them
of everything they owned, totally embitter them. They dwell
on what could have been, or, in their minds, should have
been. While it's hard to move on and to break off onto the
new paths that confront us, when you allow yourself to do
just that, you often find that what's over the horizon is pretty
spectacular. That doesn't negate the sadness of what has
happened, or the loss you feel, but you can't let those bad
feelings hold you prisoner, either. More than anything, my
faith in God has sustained me. The Lord has never let me
down, and as the Bible so wisely tells us, it is frequently in the
face of our deepest sorrows that we are given the greatest
opportunities to grow closer to Him in every way, and find
comfort in the shadow of the Almighty. I certainly have.

So here I am, on my own, and trying to approach each day
with a phrase Barbara says often: Life is not a dress rehearsal.
Once this day passes, it is over and can't be relived. Isn't that
a bittersweet notion? If I could go back, I would probably do

many things differently, react to situations differently, or avoid some things altogether! But I can't. Today is what I've got. As I move forward, hand in hand with the people I love, I try to stay in step with where I am today, rather than looking behind at what cannot be changed or ahead to the unknown. Some days it's easier said than done, but I'm getting there . . . and no matter what, even when the going gets challenging on my journey, I've got great friends and loved ones to fall back on, a new path before me filled with exciting possibilities, and some pretty fabulous shoes on my feet at all times. What more does a girl really need?

THe GLASS SLiPPeR

One of the most coveted shoes in history, worn by a princess-to-be of equal fame, is one that isn't even real—the glass slipper that transforms Cinderella from an outcast to a princess with one fell swoop . . . or fitting as the case may be.

In the familiar fairytale, Cinderella is left behind when her evil stepmother and stepsisters dash off to the royal ball without her. A fairy godmother, however, comes to Cinderella's rescue, wielding a magic wand to conjure a carriage from a pumpkin, mice into horses, and a ball gown from thin air. The crowning touch? A pair of delicate glass slippers, which set her apart from every other maiden at the ball.

More than a thousand versions and interpretations of the Cinderella story have been told or written for centuries. The first recorded version actually dates back to ninth-century China. The heroine in that story is Yeh-shen, not Cinderella. And she is helped by magical fish, not a fairy godmother. The most significant difference is the shoe. In the classic, Western version the slipper is glass. In the original Chinese story, it is golden.

On Level Ground

Growing up, my boys always looked forward to supper when they knew Mom's Famous Spaghetti Bake was on the menu. It was my secret weapon for times when dinner was delayed for this reason or that, or when Mom was just plain tired. As easy and quick as it is to put together, it's also heaven to taste: perfectly cooked spaghetti combined with a spicy, Italian meat and tomato sauce and three different kinds of cheese. You layer it in the pan, then bake it until the cheese is golden and bubbling and serve it with crusty, buttery garlic bread. Scrumptious! What my boys didn't know, of course, is that pasta is Mom's favorite comfort food, and a few of those spaghetti bake nights were just as much for me as they were for them, in more ways than one.

That's how I think of flats: They are the comfort food of shoes. Now, don't get me wrong. I love a great pair of heels as much as some women love diamonds. Seriously. When my heart needs a hug or my confidence needs a kick-start, I can slip into a pair of stacks or stilettos, and I am ready to grab a tiger by the tail! I am instantly taller, I stand straighter, and my gait becomes a confident strut. But there are also times when only a great pair of flats will suffice. I put them on when I need to navigate quickly, or when I want to let my guard down and relax. Experience has taught me, however, that you can let your guard down a little too much sometimes.

Ten years ago, after we had managed to get a couple of needlework titles successfully up and running, I realized that of all the women's lifestyles magazines I read and loved—*Martha Stewart Living* and *Victoria* among them—there was not a single title that catered to or celebrated women in the South. I knew the audience, because I *am* a Southern woman, and everywhere I went in the South, I saw so many faces, places, and untapped resources that I was sure would serve as gorgeous backdrops for a magazine. Along with the incredibly gracious women and hostesses in every small town or city, I uncovered stories that I knew needed to be told and discovered treasures I wanted to share with others: The exquisite antebellum mansions on the Battery in Charleston;

the quaint antiques shops on Royal Street in New Orleans; the hidden courtyards and gardens of Savannah . . . the list was endless.

I saw a niche that needed filling, and that's how the idea of *Southern Lady* was born. In the South, you see, being a "lady" and all that the word entails—soul-deep graciousness, generosity of spirit, and unabashed femininity—is and always has been something to aspire to. At the time, I didn't realize that it wasn't necessarily the same way in other parts of the country. To test the waters for my idea, I consulted with larger publishing houses in the South and outside of it, and I found, to my surprise, that while many people in the industry loved the idea, they were less than lukewarm about the proposed name. They told me the word "lady" in the title was newsstand poison. But my gut instinct told me the idea had legs, so I decided that only a true Southern lady could produce a magazine by the same name, and we furiously started making plans at Hoffman Media to launch the new title as a quarterly in the winter of 1999.

Now, if you ever decide to go into the periodicals publishing business for yourself, let me share an important little piece of advice with you: Readers take one look at your magazine and decide in about three seconds flat whether or not they will pick it up and buy it. The cover is everything. It has to speak to newsstand buyers and loyal subscribers who already love you, as well as readers who may not have heard about you yet, and all of this is decided in a single glance.

Certain keywords will make readers respond, as do more subtle elements, such as the type color, size, and font. Most important, however, is the cover image. To be successful, it has to offer seasonal relevance, beauty, and allow readers—especially women—to relate on a deeply emotional level. So I knew a lot was riding on the holiday issue cover of *Southern Lady*. We had already managed to put out three successful issues and word of mouth was giving us great momentum. Our 2000 Christmas issue marked the anniversary of our first year out, and the contents and cover had to be golden. *Especially* the cover.

So I looked to the original Southern lady for inspiration for the cover image: my mother, Inez Norton. Mother is gracious to the core, always putting others ahead of herself; she is deeply faithful in her spirit, and giving of herself and her many gifts in every way. She is incredibly creative, and always manages to bring a personal touch to whatever pursuit catches her interest. A painter, gifted seamstress, gardener, and cook, Mother can make something special out of *anything*, and she is forever creating beauty out of little or nothing. Her recipes are legendary, and all her friends beg for the beautiful bouquets she fashions from her own gardens. And she celebrates Christmas all year long! No matter the month or season, Mother always has a Christmas craft or project in progress, and she collects holiday recipes throughout the year to try once the season commences.

Like my Famous Spaghetti Bake, however, Mom has a few standbys she trots out every year that our whole family has come to love over time. I got the idea that Mom's world-famous Christmas cookies would make the perfect focus for the cover. I cannot remember a Christmas in my life where these cookies were not there. As I was growing up, my family always had "cookie day" during the holiday season, when we all cut out sugar cookies from the buttery chilled dough Mom had made and refrigerated the day before. Then we baked and frosted them, trying hard to leave a few for Santa. I knew those cookies would be just the magic our first Christmas cover needed, so I asked my mother for her secret, special, highly guarded recipe. Without missing a beat, she went to her pantry and tore the cover off the back of the cookie cutter box that she had saved for years with the cookies recipe printed on it and handed it to me. I had it in my hands—*the* cookie recipe. I felt like I'd just been passed the Olympic torch!

> If God sends us on strong paths, we are provided strong shoes.
> —Corrie TenBoom

Now, these days, Hoffman Media has grown, and we have stylists, editors, assistant and associate editors, test kitchen staff, photographers, color correctors—we have it all. But back then, we each wore many hats, and everything was a collective effort. Not only did I steer the company and over-see daily operations, but I had to bake the cookies for the cover of *Southern Lady* too. On an especially cold December night, I realized that the cover shoot had slipped up on me and was the next day! I grabbed the torn cookie cutter box cover and dashed to the grocery store. It was early evening, so I relaxed a little, thinking I had plenty of time to gather the ingredients, mix them up, make the dough, and let it chill overnight in the fridge. As I went down the aisles of the grocery store, I referred to the recipe often, making sure I had everything and checking off ingredients as I plopped them in my basket. I was amused that the recipe called for, among other things, "essence of vanilla." Does that tell you how old this recipe was—the term "essence of vanilla" hasn't been used in recipes since the fifties.

Later at home, I got all comfy in my nightgown, pink terrycloth robe, and matching fuzzy pink slippers. I assembled all the ingredients on the counter, got out bowls and mixers, preheated my oven, and was ready to start mixing. Except for one little problem. I couldn't find the recipe anywhere. As I tried to quell my growing sense of dread, I looked through all the grocery store sacks, every trash can in the house, my purse, my pockets, my car, my driveway, and my kitchen drawers. Nowhere. I had lost the recipe. The only copy. The secret, special, decades-old recipe was lost, and the longest-standing Norton family Christmas tradition would be broken, all because of me! That recipe had to be in the store somewhere. So I called the store and spoke to the manager. I told him this was a code-blue. The secret, special, Norton family Christmas cookie recipe was at stake. I described everything in painstaking detail: the color of the cardboard box piece and the aisles I had shopped on. He asked for my number and said he would call me back shortly.

The phone rang a little while later. No sign of the recipe. I broke out in a cold sweat and felt a tad faint. "No recipe" was not the answer I wanted to hear. Then it occurred to me that maybe I had dropped it in the parking lot. So without thinking, I ran to the car still dressed in my gown, robe, and slippers. I figured that I could circle the grocery store parking lot until I spotted the recipe, open the door, and then swoop down and pick it up without being seen. Perfect plan. It was late—around 9 PM— by this time, and I drove around the entire parking lot, now empty, but there was no recipe in sight. So I got the brilliant idea that I would retrace my steps around the parking space where I had parked earlier, in hopes that the recipe had simply fallen out of my purse as I was loading groceries. Brilliant idea. Seeing as it was dark, I got out of my car and was walking sort of bent over so I could carefully comb the area. All of a sudden, bright car lights were aimed at me—not to mention my pink fuzzy robe and matching slippers. It was the minister of music from my church. He and his family had been watching me in their car the whole time. Hearing the laughter coming from his car, I quickly got back in mine and

> I was born in high heels and I've worn them ever since.
> —Helena Christensen

offered the only explanation I could: "You won't believe it if I tell you!" Then I drove off in a hurry, admitting defeat in my head.

Lost. How could I lose the secret, special, highly guarded recipe? And more important, how could I tell my mother? How would Christmas be Christmas without those cookies? Even worse, those cookies were to be front and center in the photograph for the cover of the magazine, and the plan was already in place to shoot it the next morning; a team of photographers, stylists, florists, and more would be lined up and waiting on those cookies bright and early. T'was the night before Christmas, and all through the house, not a cookie was baking, no recipe to be found! Oh disaster! I decided to call my sister and confess. My palms were sweaty as I dialed the phone. When she answered I confessed my sin of carelessness, and she broke into hysterical, cackling laugher. She probably figured this was her chance to become the favorite child—my mistake would cement the deal. When she stopped laughing, she told me that she had copied the recipe years ago. She went and got her copy, proceeded to read it, and even recommended that I cut the cookies into snowflakes. I was back in business! That issue went on to be a success too. It was, in fact, one of the top-selling issues in the history of the magazine, but it taught me a valuable lesson about taking for granted that any plan, no matter how well thought out, will simply fall into place. Since then I've also learned to guard against getting *too* comfortable with any element of that plan (and learned the importance of making copies of recipes!) when so much is riding on the results.

Now, my friend and business associate Paula Deen would call me crazy as a Betsy Bug for saying that. Paula's favorite word (besides butter) is "comfortable," and in her case, it's paid off. The great dishes she prepares and has made famous are pure Southern comfort food: fried pork chops and chicken, soppin' gravy, biscuits, cobblers, cakes, and casseroles, to name a few. That same philosophy extends to her personality—what you see is what you get—and her wardrobe too. Most of the time, Paula romps around barefoot as can be, but if the occasion demands that she wear shoes, they are always flats. Cute little stylish flats, mind you, but flats nonetheless. In fact, I have seen Paula in heels exactly once, she wore them to a business meeting. They were a teeny-tiny little one-inch heeled pump, and I strongly suspect she was itching to get out of them the whole time.

I first met Paula in 2005, when we featured her in *Southern Lady*. That deep-down gut instinct that has always served me well told me that the same combination of good old home cooking, bubbling personality, and effervescent humor that had made Paula's cookbooks and Food Network show a success would translate into a best-selling magazine as well. I knew just from being in the room with her and seeing how others responded to Paula that her personality could carry a magazine. A publication published six times a year is like having an old friend come to visit every other month, and everyone who meets Paula wants to be her friend and get to know her better.

She first appeared as a featured columnist in our *Taste of the South* magazine, and readers were hooked in no time flat. We made the deal with Paula, hired a phenomenal staff, and settled back and relaxed, sure that her skill and talent and our publishing know-how was a recipe for success. We shouldn't have settled back on our heels so fast. Remember what I said about getting *too* comfortable? Now, you hear the phrase "overnight success" thrown around a lot these days. Let me tell you, there is rarely such an animal. In business, an "overnight success" takes about ten years. But with Paula's magazine, that concept went out the window.

We were absolutely blindsided. Almost as soon as the premier issue rolled off the press, into delivery trucks, and onto newsstand shelves, the phone calls came pouring in like an avalanche. They *kept* coming. And coming. And coming. Our lines were so flooded we had to install a new phone system to handle the sheer volume of calls. We had to outsource subscription fulfillment and customer service; we had to make at least two additional press runs of the first issue just to meet the demand. But we did it. And, this year, we brought another Food Network star, Sandra Lee, into the fold. She got her start in the crafts industry and she dominates an entirely different segment of the market with a different demographic than Paula does. *Sandra Lee Semi-*

Homemade, expanding Sandra's famous "70–30" cooking philosophy (70 percent store-bought plus 30 percent fresh ingredients) into a gorgeous lifestyle magazine that covers everything from cooking and entertaining to home decorating.

When I think about the changes my company has been through in the last ten years alone, beginning with those first humble days when I was baking cookies for the cover at home in my fuzzy pink slippers, I am overwhelmed with gratitude for my blessings and thankful all that hard work is paying off. I believe (and have learned the hard way) that in business, and in life, once you commit to something, you have to work a plan and see it through every step of the way if you want to stand tall and walk the walk. Pushing the enve lope sometimes means adjusting your comfort level, and even straying outside of it. And in my fabulous little quilted black and white flats, the ones I have come to favor on my busiest days, I have never felt more prepared or stood taller!

MOM'S FAMOUS SPAGHETTI BAKE

2 pounds ground chuck

2 cloves garlic, minced

1 green bell pepper, chopped

1 yellow onion, chopped

1 (28-ounce) can crushed tomatoes

1 (8-ounce) can tomato sauce

1 (6-ounce) can tomato paste

1 teaspoon dried oregano

1 teaspoon dried basil

1 teaspoon sugar

16 ounces uncooked linguine

1 (16-ounce) container sour cream

1 (8-ounce) package cream cheese, softened

1/2 cup chopped green onion

2 cups shredded Colby-Jack cheese

1. In a Dutch oven, brown ground chuck, garlic, bell pepper, and yellow onion over medium-high heat until meat is cooked and vegetables are tender; drain.

2. Stir in crushed tomatoes, tomato sauce, tomato paste, oregano, basil, and sugar. Reduce heat and simmer for 30 minutes.

3. In separate saucepan, cook pasta according to package directions; drain well.

4. Preheat oven to 350 degrees.

5. Place pasta in a lightly greased 13x9x9-inch baking dish. In a small bowl, combine sour cream, cream cheese, and green onion.

Spread evenly over pasta. Top with meat sauce.

6. Bake 20–25 minutes, or until heated through. Remove from oven and sprinkle Colby-Jack cheese over casserole. Bake an additional 5–10 minutes, or until cheese is melted.

NOTE: *To save time, you can substitute jarred marinara sauce with meat and vegetables. Mozzarella and Parmesan can also be substituted for the Colby-Jack.*

NORTON FAMiLY CHRiSTMAS COOKies

(Makes about 6 dozen cookies)

½ cup (1 stick) butter or margarine, softened

1 cup sugar

2 eggs

½ teaspoon vanilla extract

4 cups all-purpose flour

2 teaspoons baking powder

1 teaspoon salt

2 tablespoons milk or cream (plus 1–2 teaspoons more if needed)

Food coloring (optional)

1 recipe Cookie Icing (recipe follows)

Colored sprinkles or sanding sugar (optional)

    1. Preheat oven to 375 degrees.

    2. In a large mixing bowl, cream together butter and sugar. Add eggs one at a time, mixing well after each addition. Add vanilla extract.

3. In a separate bowl, combine flour, baking powder, and salt. Gradually add to butter mixture, mixing thoroughly. Add milk or cream (a teaspoon or two more may be added to make a smooth, moist dough). Work in food coloring, if desired. Cover dough and refrigerate for 2 or more hours.

4. On a lightly floured surface, roll dough to $1/4$–$1/2$-inch thickness. Using medium-size cookie cutters in desired shapes, cut into desired shapes. Carefully place on ungreased cookie sheets. Bake 12 minutes, or until golden brown. Cool completely.

5. Using a small spatula or butter knife, cover cookies in a thin layer of Cookie Icing, and add colored sprinkles or sanding sugar, if desired, before icing hardens .

NOTE: *Icing will dry quickly, and should harden completely.*

Cookie Icing

$1^{1}/_{2}$ cups confectioner's sugar

1 egg white

1 teaspoon vanilla extract

Food coloring (optional)

In a small bowl, whisk together confectioner's sugar, egg white, vanilla, and food coloring (if desired) until smooth. Use immediately.

CHAPTeR
11

Just Keep Walking

When I was a child, the summer season did not officially begin until all the Norton children got a new pair of flip-flops. They were play shoes to be worn outdoors only and, because they were made of rubber and foam, they could be washed spotless outside with a water hose or just tossed in the washing machine. We wore them to the beach, to the playground, and in the backyard. I never really fell in love with flip-flops because it took weeks to get used to the feeling of flossing your feet with that wretched piece of rubber that wears down the skin between your first and second toes. That blasted little piece holds the flip-flops to your feet with every step you take. Today, they are a major fashion accessory. The stores are packed full of them all year long, and they are worn with every outfit known to mortal man. I still don't get it. But I know the nail polish companies are happy as this trend has made pedicures a must-have.

In Alabama, as well as other parts of the South, warm-weather days can stretch on up into November, so flip-flops are frequent fliers with shoe buyers here; even some men wear them.

Two years ago, my precious niece, Beth, got engaged and asked if she could be married in my backyard in May. I had the privilege of making her wedding dress from beautiful pearl-colored silk with antique French lace inserts at the hem. It was just what she wanted, and she looked stunning in it. Her head piece was a wreath of tiny seed pearls. It was a vintage look that would have made Vera Wang swoon. I worked for many weeks on this dress making sure it fit properly. My mother is the master seamstress in the family, and I solicited her help in doing the "finger work," as she calls it. For those who sew, fine finger work is a point of pride; hems, linings, and the like are all sewn by hand, not machine, with small, even stitches that never show from the front of the garment. This is far more difficult than it sounds and mastering different kinds of stitches—be it slip stitches for hems or running stitches for seams—can take a lifetime to master. When it came time for the final fitting and the hemming, I told Beth to bring her shoes so we could adjust hem length and make it perfect.

Beth came to the fitting, shoes in hand. She was so excited. She had found suede flip-flops with tiny pearls on the straps, and she was just elated, saying these shoes would make the wedding ensemble complete. I shall never forget the look on my mother's face when Beth announced she would be walking down the aisle (technically through my rose garden) in flip-flops with her custom-made gown. Now my mother, "Mimi" as the grandkids call her, is a roll-with-the-flow kind of a grandmother, but flip-flops were not in the realm of her consideration, as she, like most every other Southern woman of her generation, has always favored very traditional weddings. Mimi wanted Beth to sport satin slippers or lace flats and tried to nudge her towards a more conventional shoe.

But Beth just smiled and batted her long eyelashes and Mimi knew her granddaughter's mind was made up. Beth has always considered flip-flops her signature shoe. She prides herself on being the nonconformist in the family, especially when it comes to dress. Since she is the only granddaughter on my side, her brother and four boy cousins backed her in this matter. My sister, Janice, was fine with her daughter getting married in flip-flops and announced that the bridesmaids would be wearing them as well. Mimi—who has always encouraged her children and grandchildren to enjoy life and to march to the sound of their own drummer—graciously acquiesced. When she realized that her granddaughter was intent on creating her own special day in her own special way, she laughed it off and began to tease Beth about the flip-flops instead of making them an issue or source of contention.

The big day came, and one by one, the bridesmaids trooped onward toward the pastor in their pretty dresses and bejeweled flip-flops. When Beth came down the stairs and into the garden, everyone noticed her glowing face. Her radiant smile said it all, and she was so happy; this truly was her fairytale wedding. This day was about Beth and her husband-to-be Jordan, and she had made it the wedding of her dreams. Her dreams just took a different direction from those of more traditional young Southern brides, who marry in a church in the afternoon or early evening, wearing formal dress from head to toe, followed by a reception at the local country club or fine restaurant. Did I mention that she also wanted to tie the knot at 9:30 in the morning? In fact, we had to talk her out of a sunrise ceremony. The only reason we managed to win that point is because Beth's mother (my sister Janice) is many things, but a morning person she is not. Beth is a young woman with a strong sense of confidence, and being herself is the most important thing to her. She wants everything in her life, and this included her wedding, to be a true reflection of who she is inside.

The sun was shining on that particular crisp morning in May. Friends and family were gathered and were catching up with each other. Birds were chirping, and the gentle breeze was blowing. Mom and I sat admiring our handiwork on the dress as Beth walked down the "aisle" we had created in the garden. As she strolled past us, I couldn't help but notice that Mom had hemmed the dress just a little longer than I thought it should be. As I turned to her to ask "the" question about the hem (knowing she had tried to hide the flip-flops!), she simply laughed and said, "Don't go there!" When Beth passed by her Mimi, she winked and gave her grandmother a sly, "see, I did it" look, and Mimi winked right back, no doubt thinking the same thing! They both thought they had won, but it in reality, it was a draw. Beth may have been a strong-willed bride determined to wear flip-flops with her formal, hand-sewn wedding gown, but she has a Southern grandmother who is equally sure of herself, and who is a wiz with a needle and thread! I wonder where Beth gets her spirit and tenacity?

It amazes me to see so many strong young women like Beth who are unafraid to break the rules. Do you remember when the U.S. Women's Soccer Team famously went to the White House wearing flip-flops? The whole nation was astounded, me included. But I admired their spunk, too! It takes courage to color outside the lines someone else has drawn. Consider the most well-known unwritten rule of the shoes in the South—that white shoes can never be worn after Labor Day or before Easter Sunday unless you are a bride! Why? Because my mother said so, and her mother before her, and on and on all the way back to Eve. I have often wondered who made such rules to govern our behavior and why we allow it. Perhaps someone who simply disliked white shoes? Did white shoes look bad on someone of influence years ago? Was it a manufacturing agenda? Who knows? I just know that certain rules are made to be followed, and others, well . . . at least questioned. Maybe that's why I admired Beth's unwillingness to bend to others' ideas of decorum so much. Perhaps I see a little of myself in her.

I, too, have always been unwilling to just sit back and accept the status quo; I am a person who will push the envelope or strive to break out of the mold. In fact, a dear friend (whose name is being withheld to protect the innocent but who knows *exactly* who he or she is) recently called me an "insurgent." I ran to the dictionary in my office and looked up the exact definition: "A person who revolts against civil authority; a rebel not recognized as a belligerent." I snapped the dictionary shut with glee. That's me all over—a rebel who can color inside the lines as well as the next person . . . as long as I can kick the lines with my exquisitely pointed heels in any direction I choose whenever I like!

I started out as the firstborn, the experimental child, the one who pioneered the way for the siblings that followed. I went to work as a CPA at a firm where I knew only a handful of people, taking full financial responsibility for myself, and beginning a career in what had traditionally been a man's profession. It didn't dawn on me at the time that I would be one in the first wave of women in accounting, but I found out fast that I was treading in waters that had not been disturbed by high heels before! A few years later, I started over as someone's wife, complete with a new last name, a new address, and a new identity. Three years later, twins! And I started over as a mother. After that, my path took yet another detour, this time leading me into a new career that would reap unimagined rewards, and a few sleepless nights too.

Are you at a place of starting over or in the throes of unexpected change? I can tell you that fear sometimes grips our hearts at the thought of beginning a new phase of life, taking a path we didn't plan on, or seizing an opportunity that presents itself. But that's the dividing line, isn't it? Our lives can change with a phone call, a letter, a conversation, or a doctor's visit, and we find ourselves walking a path we hadn't dreamed of and haven't prepared for. When the choice is made without our consent, then we walk a path of uncertainty and many times are guided by fear. I would never choose to wear a pair of shoes that would take me down a path of hurt and disappointment, and never would I choose a path of loneliness of my own volition. When these uncertain paths become

inevitable and must be tread, I
have tried to face them with
the idea that I will become a
stronger person by taking
this journey. I urge you to
do the same. At any time
during your walk, you may
need a person to walk with

you. Two sets of footprints make the walk easier and at times
make the walk shorter.

A dear friend and confidante of mine, a fellow Southern
girl whose name you may know, Nancy Grace, likes to
recount the story of a race that her friend entered. Her friend
had signed up for a half marathon and found herself in the
wrong race. She was in a full marathon and had to make a
choice. She could drop out or she could run. So she ran. She
finished the race too!

Nancy also tells the story of an event that changed her
life. It happened while she was still in college. Her fiancé,
Keith, was murdered before they could marry, and all the
plans she had made for her life went out the window. Today,
Nancy is one of the country's leading figures on criminal jus-
tice and hosts an award-winning news commentary show
where she goes to bat for victims. Onscreen she is one tough
cookie, but off-screen she is a gentle and loving wife and a
mother of twins. The life she is living today is wonderful,
but it isn't necessarily the one she originally had planned for

herself. She wasn't given an option. Her life was all mapped
out when a single gunshot changed everything.

But that experience, and the ones that followed, have led
Nancy to happiness and fulfillment today because she didn't
just give up and sit down. She kept going, and now she is
blessed with an exciting career and a beautiful family to show
for her perseverance. There is a phrase that Nancy frequently
repeats, sort of a personal mantra for her that is deeply mean-
ingful to me as well: "It may not be the race you chose, but
it is the race you are in—so run!" That's what I'm doing. I'm
running for all I'm worth, occasionally stopping to reflect on
where I am in the race, where I have been, and where I am
heading next. At this moment, I am facing life as a woman
who has survived many unexpected ups and downs in life
and business. I'm wondering what is coming next, and
excited about what's around the corner or just over the horizon! I am, after all, a person who can tolerate a great deal of
change and adversity, but not even one second of boredom.
I thirst for new adventures the same way I long for a new pair
of shoes, and I seek both out every day.

Though you might imagine that I'm a lot like Princess Di
with hundreds of pairs of shoes in my closet, I'm not. I love
new shoes more than anything, but I know my closet can only
hold so many, so every so often I take stock of what is there.
Like every other woman I know, I inevitably discover shoes I
had forgotten I even had—styles that are no longer in vogue,
others that don't fit, or are worn out from too much wear.

There are many pairs of those wonderful show-and-tell "valet shoes" reserved for special occasions; the all-business black pumps and red boardroom-ready slingbacks I adore; the many shoes I shopped for with my dearest friends; the flats I love on can't-slow-down days, and yes, there are a few questionable choices in there too. But for better or for worse, in style and back out again, these shoes belong to me. They're mine.

Don't waste time regretting the shoes you chose; keep your mind trained on the shoes you're wearing while allowing yourself to dream of the next pair you might pick up. You know the famous Nike athletic shoe slogan, "Just Do It"? Those are words to live by. Whatever shoes are on your feet today, just wear them. Celebrate who you are in those shoes! If nothing else, I promise, you will have the absolute satisfaction of knowing *you* chose them. And honey, take it from me, when you wear those shoes, wear them with attitude; wear them with style. It will make all the difference.

WEDDING SHOES

The first pair of high heels ever worn in recorded history belonged to a bride—not to mention one of the most famously celebrated women in history, Catherine de' Medici. When the Italian teenager walked down the aisle in 1533 to marry Henry II of France, she wore a pair of high heels that had been made for her in her native Florence. Hitherto, only men were known to wear elevated shoes.

Madame de' Medici was only fourteen years old when she wed the heir to the throne of France; it was a marriage deemed by the Pope himself as "the greatest match in the world." As the future king's Queen Consort, Italy's diminutive "Little Duchess" set off a fashion firestorm in the French court with her adored high heels. Catherine was known to add five or more inches to her height with heels, and the swaying gait that wearing them caused made her a style sensation. A famed patron of the arts and icon of elegance, Catherine is credited not only for bringing high heels to fashion in France, but also the wearing of corsets and perfume.

AFTERWORD

Private Collection

I like to keep my shoe collection capped at around 100 pairs. When my shoe closet gets full to overflowing, I know it's time to dig in there and separate the wheat from the chaff, so to speak. Some I give to friends and some of my most prized possessions I share with my beautiful daughter-in-law, Katie, who loves shoes as much as I do, and who wears the same size. I am so glad my son, Eric, fell in love with her, she and I were like a pair of perfectly matched shoes from the beginning. Others I retire to their final resting place, where all shoes past their prime eventually end up, and some I simply won't give away for love or money. It's not easy to pick my "favorite" shoes because I adore them all! But here are my Top Ten—some because they hold great sentimental value for me and others just because they're so wonderful I can't bear to part with them!

Brown Satin Slingbacks: MOG Shoes

My brown satin slingback pumps (complete with rhine-
stones on the toe!) signify one of the most important events
of my life: The day I officially became a MOG—the mother
of the groom. My MOG shoes were the perfect choice to
complement the brown satin evening gown that I had carefully selected for Eric and Katie's wedding. These are
significant shoes for me; I have only worn them
once. But look what I got in return for wearing
them: a beautiful daughter-in-law, a wonder-
fully happy son, and a year later, an unbeliev-
able grandson. But before all *that*, before the
wedding, I was still a MOG determined to
put my best foot forward in this new relationship.

Now, could we all stop here for a moment and think about
all the awful mother-in-law jokes that we have all heard so
many times? I was determined that when my title changed
from MOG to MIL (mother-in-law), my name would be
cleared of any such wrongdoings, but I must say, setting
about to be a model MIL was a real challenge. I heard my
minister say the most perfect thing that clearly defines the
situation: "Problems usually arise when we have two women
who are in love with the same man." Well, what a genius! Of
course, I have been in love with my twin sons since they were
conceived. I love being a boy mom . . . it just has fun written
all over it. And up until this point, I had always been *the*
woman in their lives.

That all changed when Eric met Katie. When I met her, they were still dating, and immediately, I knew there was something special about this young lady. More important, I knew she was the one for my Eric. His countenance was different. He had a smile most of the time. When they were together, time seemed to pass quickly, and each word spoken between them just reinforced to me that they were meant to be together. A few weeks after our first meeting, Eric called to say he was in love with Katie and he wanted to marry her. At last! I would have a daughter-in-law; I was completely beside myself. He selected the ring and planned how he would propose to her. She said yes, and it was just magic, exactly like Eric wanted it to be.

As the weeks progressed, we were working on the details of the wedding, but as the MOG, my main responsibility was the rehearsal dinner. This was my chance to shine! The dinner would be a dream-come-true, and I would give it my best to make it perfect for Eric and Katie. They selected the menu they wanted, and we decided to use the blue theme that she loved. All was moving along just fine with the dinner plans and decorations. I had even recorded a piano CD of their favorite music to be played during the event.

Then it came time for me to order invitations for the rehearsal dinner. I had found the most wonderful young woman who handmade them, and I was just elated when she wanted to do ours. She sent me some ideas, and the one that I loved the most was silk with a monogrammed motif. Monograms are my passion. I just love them on everything; I have even been accused of monogramming my socks! I shared this glorious find with Katie and Eric and could not wait for the thrilled reaction I was expecting. They seemed so delighted with my creativity and desire to do the unusual. However, a couple of days later, Eric came to me and said, "Mom, Katie is not sure that she wants the monogram on the invitations. It just really isn't her." I just sat in disbelief. What? No monograms—*the* hallmark of the publisher of *Southern Lady* magazine? I started to plead my case and then stopped.

I looked into Eric's eyes and saw this wonderful young man who was trying to figure out a way to make both of the women in his life happy. The look he had on his face was overwhelming to me. I realized that my son was in the position of having to choose between the love of his life and his mother. That is a no-win situation for anybody. While he knew that having monograms would thrill me beyond words, his Katie didn't want them. As I continued to look into his eyes, I also knew my response to this situation would set the tone for the remainder of our lives together as a family. Eric stood there waiting on my response. I could see the years yet to come in his eyes, and his own immediate family's future as well. It was one of those moments I will remember forever. I smiled and said, "No monograms."

He hugged me with the greatest hug I believe he has ever given me. It wasn't about the monograms; it was about loving him and letting him go, so he could love his new bride unconditionally. Katie knew that day that she was number one, and what woman doesn't want to know that in her life? The invitations were perfect, even without monograms! A few weeks later, Katie was gorgeous, and Eric was so handsome at the rehearsal dinner. I marveled at what a splendid couple they made and how their future could only hold happiness and great joy. Both families rejoiced as we all fell in love with one another. This was a mother's dream for her son.

From the time he proposed to Katie, I had continually asked him, "Eric, do you love Katie more than me?" I loved watching him squirm as he tactfully told me that this was a different kind of love. Every so often, I would ask the same question, and I always got the same response and smile. We would laugh, and I realized that this one man loved two women deeply, and how lucky I was to be one of them.

The day of the wedding finally arrived. Right before the service as we were all lining up for the procession, I asked Eric for the last time if he loved Katie more than me. He smiled his charming smile at me and said, "Yes Mom, I do!" I shot back, "Then you are ready to get married!" His brother Brian escorted me down the aisle in my brown satin slingback shoes, and I took my place on the second row in the church. When Eric and Katie said "I do," I went from MOG to MIL and gained, in the process, a brand new daughter-in-law to love like she was my own.

Red Shoes: Wearing Your Heart on Your Heel

Once I bought my first pair of red shoes, I knew I was addicted for life. They reflect what's really going on in my heart. I have a thirst for excitement and daring. Red is the color that reflects my passion for life.

Cruella De Vil Shoes: Sass with Class

Because I have so many different business meetings to attend, I usually wear a black suit. To throw everyone completely off guard, I put on a stunning pair of shoes, like my Cruella De Vil shoes, or something just as sassy.

Tangerine Stacks: The Shoes of the Magi

This past Christmas, my daughter-in-law Katie and I were shopping in New York City and stumbled upon the most incredible pair of Anne Klein shoes. Right in the middle of all these dark and somber shoes of winter sat these glorious tangerine-colored stacks with a matching leather flower on the toe. They were *calling* to us.

We both circled them like seagulls waiting to snatch a fish from the ocean, while warring with ourselves, saying we didn't *need* orange shoes right now. I watched her eyeing those summery shoes while trying on tall winter boots with stiletto heels, and I decided that those tangerine heels would be under the tree for Katie on Christmas morning. She purchased her boots and we lingered as we left the store, passing by "our shoes" one last time. Since we wear the same size, we always know that if one of us has a great pair, the other does too. But purchasing them then would have killed the element of surprise. I decided to wait until I got home to Alabama, when I could call and have the shoes shipped.

When I returned home, I called that department store many times, always being put on eternal hold, and could not get anyone to assist me. I couldn't *believe* that such a major department store would miss a sale with such poor customer service. My final attempt resulted in a *forty-five-minute* holding pattern resulting in no assistance.

Our family Christmas celebration came, and I was so disappointed that I couldn't have the shoes for Katie to unwrap. When it came time to open my gifts, Katie told me that my main gift was being shipped. Katie had persevered and had purchased those fabulous Anne Klein shoes for me, and they were somewhere in the Christmas packages being shipped all over the country.

I was delighted! If people didn't know better, they would swear she was my daughter, because if I had to custom-order one, Katie would be it. I will wear those shoes, with great memories of our Big Apple trip, and always remember the time and effort she put into surprising me. Isn't that what life is really about, making dreams come true for the people we love? Going the extra mile to bring pleasure to someone is so rewarding. Sometimes that road is easy to walk and sometimes it takes great effort, but knowing I have such loving and giving people in my life who go to such lengths to please me blesses me so much! So in the same spirit, I tracked down another pair of those splendid shoes online just after Christmas. I ordered them for Katie, and now we each have our own. The shoes of the Magi, indeed!

Ebony and Ivory: When You Can't Decide

My most unusual pair of shoes is the half-black, half-white shoe. I love these shoes because they catch people by surprise. I'm a sucker for two-toned shoes: I love spectators and cap-toe heels. I got these at Nordstrom's in Tampa.

Wall Street Shoes with Bling: Business with Attitude

I liked these shoes the minute I saw them because of the unusual combination of glen plaid wool fabric and a red rhinestone brooch on the toe. I don't wear them often, but every time I do, I think they convey a strong message: "I am business with attitude."

Orange Pumps: Santa Shoes

My son Brian is always up to mischief. At Christmastime, Brian would always pull a fast one on me. When he was a little boy and wanting to test the waters regarding the authenticity of Old Saint Nick, he would conjure up a "test" to see if Santa was real or not. This had become a pattern. One year, Brian asked Santa to wrap all of his and his brother Eric's gifts in paper with Santa's picture on it. Thank goodness the local drug store was open until midnight! After the boys fell asleep, I made an emergency run to collect all the Santa paper in the store, and much of it is still hidden somewhere in my basement to this day. After that near miss, I vowed never to be caught again with one of Brian's tests!

The next year, on Christmas Eve—and well after all stores were closed, mind you—Brian came and sat on my lap and whispered in my ear, "I have a test to see if Santa is real. I've asked him to bring you a pair of shoes for Christmas, but I've made it really hard. I've asked for a color that I haven't seen—orange! If it happens than I'll know he's real. If not, then I will know that too." I told him that Santa was too consistently fashion savvy to fall for that one, that he simply would not bring out-of-season shoes.

But this year, he really thought he had outsmarted Santa.

Little did my son know that I was a step ahead of him. I had recently been to North Carolina to visit my friend Barbara and we, of course, had been shoe shopping. The new spring colors were out, and you guessed it; I had bought the coolest pair of orange kitten heel pumps and had tucked them away, in the top of my closet, completely out of sight. What luck! On Christmas morning, Brian woke up first and raced to the family room to see if there were orange shoes with my name on them. Near the fireplace was a beautifully wrapped box addressed to "Mom," and inside were the orange shoes. His little eyes gazed in amazement and he laughed with delight. "Can you *believe* he knew your perfect size? I didn't tell him that!"

The next spring, I pulled out all the stops with those fun shoes, thinking of my son's perfect, childlike belief in Santa Claus with every step. When I wore them, Brian would smile and would say, "Got your Santa shoes on today!" I always had the same reply: "Next year, ask for a large diamond ring!"

Saddle Leather Slingbacks: A Little Bit Country

Country music stars and Texans have a definite flair when it comes to their attire. Made of saddle leather with a ruffled bow and accented with brads, these shoes look great with jeans and give me just the right amount of panache when I want a casual look.

Printed Patterned Pumps: Sticking Your Neck Out for Style

These are giraffe print piped in red. They have tall heels, and they must be worn with a very plain outfit because the shoes are the outfit.

Organists' Shoes: Pedal to the Metal

If you have ever seen an organist play, you might wonder why the instrument is played with both the feet and the hands. Such is the glory of the organ. The soft-soled shoes you wear to play it are designed for toe-heel technique in playing the pedals of the organ; they are not made to make a fashion statement.

In the twenty-five years that I have played, I have provided organ music for church services, weddings, funerals, and many other events. A preacher once told me that good organ playing is like good stick bologna: "It doesn't matter where you cut it off, it's the same." After I thought about it, I told him that I had decided when I had heard all the sermon I wanted, I would start playing the closing hymn whether he was finished or not. We had a great working relationship from that day forward.

My organists' shoes have taken me to some wonderful places that have allowed me to share in other people's most life-changing events, weddings in particular. Some have been flawless and others . . . not-so-flawless. One story that sticks in my mind occurred at the wedding of my dear friends George and Sally (full disclosure here: The names are definitely changed to protect me!). I had known them since high school, and we even attended the same college.

Their wedding was one of those weddings to which everyone who was anyone in Birmingham had been invited. And it seemed most of them were there. The church was very large with the organ situated right down in front, so that the congregation could see every note the organist played. It was not the church where I regularly played, so this was a new experience for me. Normally I wasn't center stage, but instead, played from a sunken alcove inside the choir loft where no one could see anything but the top of my head. That set-up suited me just fine, thank you very much!

As the countdown to the walk down the aisle began, I slid onto the bench just in time to start the prelude (thirty minutes of "warm-up music," as it is referred to by my children) with not a minute to spare. A charming young lady who was interpreting for the deaf came up and asked if she could borrow my music to write the words so she could follow along with sign language as the soloist sang. I nodded and kept playing. She returned my music to its proper place, and the prelude continued.

Right after George and Sally's mothers were seated, it was time for the first solo. The oversized, incredible tenor, Roy, broke into song with all the gusto he could muster: "Because

God Made Thee Mine." Now, in the seventies, this was not in the playlist of songs that I would want at any wedding, much less the wedding of my friends. Right at the pinnacle point of this song when the highest and loudest notes were being sung, I turned the page of my music, only to find the middle page of "The Lord's Prayer." The interpreter has accidentally shuffled the pages.

I turned to Roy and said in my loudest stage whisper "I don't have the right music!" He kept right on singing and started walking toward me, putting his music right down in front of me without missing a note. It was in a different key! I turned again and said, "Stop singing," while I quickly got to the key written. We somehow managed to finish the song and I glanced over at the mother of the bride, who was staring holes through me. Clearly, she was not amused.

Suddenly, Roy realized he had forgotten to turn on a cassette player to record the wedding as he had promised George and Sally. I looked out of the corner of my eye and saw this large black robe draped over Roy . . . who was *crawling* through the choir loft to hit the "record" button. Finally he got close enough, hit the button to turn on the cassette player, and proceeded to back out of the choir loft. As he got to the end, the hem of his robe caught on tall candelabra. It fell, crashing into the next candelabra and so on, and so on. They all came crashing down like dominos! I was the only one who could see him and was so tickled, it was all I could do to contain my laughter. No one in the church even knew Roy was in the choir loft. While biting the inside of my cheeks trying not to laugh out loud, the mother of the bride looked at me and said, "Play something!" While trembling inside with laughter, I intoned with soft meditative music, while the florist reassembled the candles so the wedding could continue.

At last, all was back in order; then it was time for the bride to make her grand entrance. I brought up the organ to full decibel level, and in came Sally in all of her glory, wearing a gorgeous dress complete with an antique Brussels lace veil that her mother had been saving for this special day. She beamed as she walked down the aisle to meet George, the love of her life. As they were preparing to move up onto the stage, the usual questions were asked with the programmed responses of "I do," and "Her mother and I." As Sally took her first step forward to take her groom's hand, her head snapped back, and that exquisite lace veil went whooshing off her crown and onto the floor. George was standing on it.

The mother of the bride, who I suspected was already at her breaking point, arose from her pew quick as a flash. She dashed to the stage, yanked the veil up off the ground, and proceeded to pin it back in place. While she was up there, she decided she might as well straighten the train of the dress too. When she bent over to adjust the train, her too-tight, powder-blue, full-length satin suit made a terrible ripping sound. And at that moment, when her zipper completely gave way, the mother of the bride had her backside to every wedding guest in the place.

I was out of control now, holding my head down as tears of laughter came streaming down my face. Is there anything worse that completely getting tickled in church? No, nothing at all. My face was red, my hands were sweaty. While I struggled to maintain *some* composure, Sally's mother made a quick, strategic decision. She left the front of the church and went back to her seat, ripped suit and all. The wedding continued. The couple had made their way to the altar on the upper platform of the stage. During the prayer, the flower girl (don't have children in your wedding) decided it was her turn to perform, and she turned to her mother and yelled, "Hey mama!" Sally turned to look and see what all the noise was about, and when she did, the antique Brussels lace veil brushed the altar candle and caught fire. The Minister was patting the fire out and praying at the same time.

When that prayer was finished and all was said and done, they were pronounced man and wife. I started the recessional to lead them out of the sanctuary. Sally stopped to give George's mother a flower from her bouquet, then turned to her mother to do the same. The mother of the bride rose again from her seat, looked at George and said, "You will pay for this for the rest of your life!" And I am quite certain that he has.

As soon as the last note had sounded, I quickly gathered my things and ran to my car as fast as I could. I have never seen either of my friends again. They have not attended any high school reunions, nor have they responded to any invitations. But every so often, when I put on my organist's shoes to play, I think about how real life can be better than television, and when I play for a wedding these days I hold my breath and hope that history doesn't repeat itself!

iNDeX

ABOUT THE AUTHOR

A leading figure in the publishing industry, Phyllis Norton Hoffman is president and chief executive officer of Hoffman Media, LLC. A native of Alabama and a graduate of the University of Alabama in Birmingham, she began her career as a Certified Public Accountant with a nationally known firm before founding a special-interest publication company in 1983 that is now known as Hoffman Media, LLC.

Hoffman is recognized industry-wide as a savvy business-woman and talented entrepreneur. Whether the topic is the enjoyment and rituals of tea or the basic Southern hospitality her region is known for, she is eloquent in her leadership role. She serves as the creative engine of the company she founded that produces the magazines that define and celebrate women's lifestyles, including *Sandra Lee Semi-Homemade, Cooking with Paula Deen, Victoria, TeaTime, Southern Lady, Taste of the South, Just CrossStitch,* and *Sew Beautiful.* Hoffman has also published and authored several Southern-inspired entertaining and decorating books including *Southern Lady: Gracious Spaces, Southern Lady: Gracious Tables,* and *The Entertaining Touch.*

Sought after as a speaker across the country, Hoffman is also a devoted mother and grandmother, and a church and community leader.